Lynda Roscoe Hartigan 12/31/79

THE DRAWINGS OF
MORRIS LOUIS

THE DRAWINGS OF
MORRIS LOUIS

Published for the
National Collection of Fine Arts
by the Smithsonian Institution Press
Washington, D.C.
1979

Published on the occasion of an exhibition organized by the National Collection of Fine Arts and shown at

National Collection of Fine Arts
Smithsonian Institution
Washington, D.C.
December 6, 1979–February 3, 1980

Fogg Art Museum
Harvard University
Cambridge, Massachusetts
February 22–April 6, 1980
With assistance from The Northeastern Pooled Common Fund for Education in the Social Sciences and the Arts

Library of Congress Cataloging in Publication Data
Louis, Morris, 1912–1962.
    The drawings of Morris Louis.
    Text by D. U. Headley.
    Exhibition held at National Collection of Fine Arts, Smithsonian Institution, Washington, Dec. 6, 1979–Feb. 3, 1980 and at Fogg Art Museum, Harvard University, Cambridge, Mass., Feb. 22–April 6, 1980.
    Includes bibliographical references.
    1. Louis, Morris, 1912–1962 — Exhibitions. I. Headley, Diane Upright. II. Smithsonian Institution. National Collection of Fine Arts. III. Harvard University. William Hayes Fogg Art Museum. IV. Title.
NC139.L59A4   1979   741.9′73   79-607806

For sale by the Superintendent of Documents
United States Government Printing Office
Washington, D.C. 20402
Stock number: 047–003–00067–9

Frontispiece: Untitled, catalogue number D494 [1948–49], pen and ink and gouache on paper.

Photographic Credits

Archives of American Art, Smithsonian Institution, Washington, D.C.: *Sketches for Tanktotem III*, p. 51.
The Art Institute of Chicago, Illinois: *Woman with a Helmet of Hair*, p. 23, *Cyclops*, p. 58.
The Baltimore Museum of Art, Maryland: *The Pink Nude*, p. 40.
André Emmerich Gallery, New York: *Delta Kappa*, p. 61; Malcolm Varon, photographer: *Phi*, p. 61.
Diane Upright Headley: pp. 15–19.
Hirshhorn Museum and Sculpture Garden, Smithsonian Institution, Washington, D.C.: *Water Figure*, p. 35.
The Metropolitan Museum of Art, New York: *The Dark Mountain No. 2*, p. 26.
The Museum of Modern Art, New York: *Self-Portrait*, p. 32, *Minotauromachy*, p. 37, *Portrait of Mistress Mills in 1750*, p. 47, *Study for Nighttime Enigma and Nostalgia*, p. 48, *Objects*, p. 48, *The Hunter (Catalan Landscape)*, p. 50.

CONTENTS

FOREWORD

There can be few more significant instances of the importance of drawings for understanding the true nature of an artist's creative accomplishment than that provided by the drawings of Morris Louis. Since his work initially became known only through paintings created when he was already in his forties, and these could be related quite readily to tendencies then current, Louis's subtle, abstract canvases have more often been seen as existing in a context of schools and critical premises than in the context of his own creative life. There is no question that the paintings executed during the last ten years or so of his career are his most notable achievements, justifying his place among the major painters of the time, but they are the culmination of a long and complex process of introspection and artistic experiment. They did not spring as spontaneously to his hand as they did to the critical eye. The seeming ease with which his mature paintings emerge into life can easily be misread. Effortlessness was the ultimate reward of concentration and discipline, of private thought and patient searching.

This long and explorative process is well documented in his largely unpublished drawings, which served as the primary arena for the development of Louis's visual thinking. Far ranging in kind and direction, they reveal a questioning, probing mind that was not hampered by formal programs or doctrinaire premises. It is noteworthy that Louis's drawings are not devoted to trying out effective modes of presentation or improvising on formal effects; they are, instead, explorations into the nature of artistic content as he understood it, deeply rooted in the mind. That forms take shape as a necessary part of the personal engagement in thought and feeling was basic to Louis's commitment as an artist. Nowhere is this more clearly stated than in his profoundly personal drawings.

We are much indebted to Marcella Louis Brenner for bringing these drawings to our attention and agreeing to their exhibition and publication, and to Diane Upright Headley for the perceptive study of their content.

Joshua C. Taylor, *Director*
National Collection of Fine Arts

ACKNOWLEDGMENTS

This publication and the exhibition it accompanies were made possible by the generosity and cooperation of a great many individuals. Foremost among them is Marcella Louis Brenner, the artist's widow, who made available most of the drawings included in this project and offered her encouragement and advice whenever they were needed. Joshua C. Taylor's enthusiastic response to the exhibition proposal and his suggestion that the accompanying publication include a catalogue raisonné of the drawings set the project on its way. André Emmerich greatly facilitated my research and this publication by photographing all the drawings in the Louis estate. Bayat Keerl is to be thanked for his able photographic work. Mr. I. S. Weissbrodt assisted me during my research on the material in the Louis estate archives.

Many of Morris Louis's friends and acquaintances were generous with their time by granting me interviews or corresponding with me. In this regard I would like to thank Stephens Berge, Mr. and Mrs. Stanley Blumberg, Leonard Bocour, Adelyn Breeskin, Mervin Jules, Chet LaMore, Herman Maril, Charles Schucker, William Spiegel, and Sam Swerdloff.

I am also grateful to the following lenders to the exhibition: Mrs. Jeannette Kear, Mrs. Moses Siegel, Andrew Bradford Smith, and William Spiegel; and The Maryland Institute, College of Art.

Finally, in the Department of Prints and Drawings at the National Collection of Fine Arts, Janet Flint and her assistant, Martina Norelli, helped me at every stage, providing not only their very able skills but also a warm and friendly place to work.

Diane Upright Headley

THE DRAWINGS OF
MORRIS LOUIS

by Diane Upright Headley
Department of Fine Arts
Harvard University

Even for some of his most fervent admirers, the career of Morris Louis has presented certain difficulties since the early 1960s, when the high level of his achievement first began to be acknowledged. The primary problem stemmed from the fact that remarkably little was known about Louis or his career prior to the exhibition of his 1961–62 Stripe paintings, the last paintings he executed before his death. His career spanned three decades; he worked mostly in Baltimore and Washington, cities viewed as provincial outposts by the New York art community. Only after Louis's death did any interest begin to emerge in his earlier paintings, a change spurred by his memorial exhibition at the Guggenheim Museum in 1963. Lawrence Alloway focused that exhibition on the series of Veil and Floral paintings Louis executed between 1954 and 1959, works that had gone relatively unnoticed when Clement Greenberg had presented them in two sizeable exhibitions in New York City at French & Company in 1959 and 1960. When Alan Solomon selected thirteen of Louis's pictures for the Venice Biennale of 1964, his choices constituted the first survey of paintings from all of Louis's mature series: the Veils, Florals, Unfurleds, and Stripes. This biennale group provided the model for a small retrospective that toured Europe in 1965.

Michael Fried assumed the responsibility in 1967 for Louis's first comprehensive American retrospective and wrote a pioneering essay for the exhibition catalogue. For the first time, Louis's mature paintings were supplemented by his early work; a dozen of the fifty-four pictures shown dated from 1939–53. Fried's essay, however, dismissed the early paintings as "both minor and provincial," despite his expressed conviction that by the late 1940s Louis was an accomplished painter. Fried was profoundly impressed by the nature of Louis's achievement after 1954, which he viewed as "a repudiation of and revulsion against [the earlier] work and its underlying assumptions," a change that constituted a breakthrough to "not just a new kind of painting, but [to] his own artistic identity as well." Examination of the group of early paintings to which Fried refers reveals clearly that his conclusions are valid. Louis was neither an exceptional nor original painter during the first twenty years of his professional career.

When the focus is shifted away from the early paintings to Louis's drawings from those same years, however, the terms repudiation and revulsion no longer accurately characterize the relationship between the pre- and post-1954 work. Louis's drawings reveal an inventive, emotionally rich, and complex imagery as well as a sensitivity of draftsmanship that were brought to fruition in his mature paintings. In the drawings we can observe in a concrete manner the breadth of sensibility that pulses through the core of his successful later paintings. The drawings also clarify the sources, both artistic and personal, whose absorption and distillation provide a partial substructure for his subsequent achievement. The incredible ease and fluidity often characteristic of his pen prepared him, as his early efforts with a brush neither did nor could have done, for the possibilities inherent in the technique of pouring paint across huge expanses of canvas. The pleasure that drawing afforded him and, equally, the discipline he imposed on his facility are features shared with the best of his mature paintings. Also evident in both groups of work is Louis's compulsion to push an idea as far as possible, to explore every nuance before pursuing another goal. Obviously, however, certain crucial aspects of the mature paintings could only have resulted from lessons absorbed during the painting process, especially the mastery of large scale and coloristic richness.

The introduction of Louis's drawings to the known body of his oeuvre expands our comprehension of his achievement in far more than a simple quantitative sense. It permits us to grasp the totality of his achievement, to comprehend that the brief period during which he produced so many excellent paintings was neither an accident of history nor a superficial response to events that immediately preceded this period. Quite the contrary, for Louis's career, like that of so many of the abstract expressionists who were his contemporaries, was marked by a prolonged period of apprenticeship that contained within it the seeds of future greatness. That later achievement is not amplified but is, in fact, weakened by dissociation from its period of germination. Certainly one would not seize upon an artist's first childhood doodlings as prefigurations of his mature art, yet one cannot fully comprehend that maturity by divorcing it from its origins. In the case of Morris Louis we are particularly fortunate to possess a sizeable oeuvre of drawings from the crucial period during which he chose, and eventually extricated himself from, alignments with key masters of twentieth-century art. As a result, the assessment of Louis's career by future historians will be inexorably strengthened.

PROFESSIONAL DEVELOPMENT, 1927–1946

Morris Bernstein, who later adoped the name Morris Louis, was born in Baltimore in 1912, the third of four sons of an ambitious immigrant family. The eldest brother was a physician and the second a pharmacist; the family was struggling to raise tuition money to put the youngest through medical school when Morris made a career decision that profoundly distressed his parents. At the age of fifteen he decided to become an artist and entered the Maryland Institute of Art on a four-year scholarship. During his stay at this staunch bastion of academic training, Louis was only a slightly better than average student. He was awarded a diploma by the fine arts department in 1932.[1]

During the 1920s and 1930s, the conservatism of the Maryland Institute of Art was echoed by the city's other art institutions, making it extremely difficult for artists with avant-garde leanings to pursue their interests or, for that matter, even to see good examples of nonacademic art. The Walters Art Gallery was still a private collection, only occasionally open to the public. The Baltimore Museum of Art opened in 1923, but its exhibitions for many years were overwhelmingly conservative in nature, accurately reflecting the taste of its visitors.

That one of the country's most important collections of modern European art, the rapidly expanding Cone Collection, was housed in Baltimore was not appreciated nor even acknowledged by most residents, nor even by most members of the museum's staff. Baltimoreans who were aware of the activities of Dr. Claribel and Miss Etta Cone regarded the sisters as slightly insane. According to the recollections of Dr. George Boas, who joined the faculty of Johns Hopkins in 1921 to teach philosophy, "I was warned that of course I might visit the Cone Collection if I wished, but that its owners were beyond doubt mental cases."[2] He was not deterred and, in fact, enjoyed many visits to the Cones' apartments; he became somewhat of a liaison between the Cones and young Baltimore artists who learned from him about the collection and occasionally received invitations to view it.[3]

One such visitor, a student at the Maryland Institute of Art named Shelby Shackelford, became the center of a controversy that demonstrates the problems encountered by imaginative art students in the city at that time.[4] She had won a scholarship to paint abroad for a year and returned in 1925 with the expectation of exhibiting the work produced, one of the stipulations of the prize. The modernity of the paintings so offended the institute's director, Hans Shuler, however, that he cancelled the exhibition. A local piano teacher provided the needed space and the work was shown and given full, though negative, press coverage. Four years later, when Dr. Claribel Cone died and her will was reported in the *Baltimore Sun,* it was evident that she was not convinced that Baltimoreans had yet broadened their view of art; she left her collection initially to her sister and eventually to the Baltimore Museum on the condition that "the spirit of appreciation of modern art in Baltimore should improve." Upon Etta Cone's death in 1949 the situation had changed sufficiently for her to bequeath the entire collection to the museum.

We are most fortunate to be able to place Morris Louis in the context of Baltimore's art community and the Maryland Institute of Art during this period through the recollections of Charles Schucker, a painter who was then Louis's closest friend.[5] Although four years older than Louis, Schucker entered the institute in 1928 and met Louis soon thereafter. Within a year they had become best friends both in school and out, for they lived within walking distance of each other on Baltimore's west side.[6] Schucker recalls that Louis, like his brothers, was "fairly tense, animated and very bright," a heavy smoker, a loner who had no other close friends, and a man already totally committed to his art despite his family's reservations. "His family didn't understand anything he was trying to do. Morris and I were sort of freaks to the family, but they were nice about it," Schucker has remarked.

The two young men shared an interest in color that was not reciprocated by their fellow students nor by the faculty members. Schucker remembers that Louis had a "natural facility or talent, a feeling for paint and for color in relation to the surfaces" — this despite a "built-in handicap; one of the saving graces of his talent: he couldn't realize, he couldn't make anything." Such a handicap, confirmed by the awkwardnesses of Louis's extant early figurative paintings, obviously posed a serious problem in a school that followed the beaux-arts practice of progressing from drawing plaster casts through carefully regulated stages until students were finally permitted to work from live models. Louis apparently tried to overcome his difficulties by a habit developed at this time and evident in his work for the rest of his career. As Schucker describes it, "When he'd get interested in something he'd practically wear it out. He had this ability to select something and stick to it. For example, when he was trying to make one figure sit in a space, he'd do twenty or thirty versions with hardly any difference between them." This description applies not only to Louis's drawings from the 1940s and early 1950s, but also to his mature paintings where the differences between the works in a given series often reflect a subtle process of refinement rather than radical change.

To make up for the deficiencies they perceived in their education, which included only one art appreciation course to supplement studio classes, Schucker and Louis went to the library. One of their earliest discoveries was the work of Eugene Speicher (1883 – 1962), a portrait painter trained at the Art Students League by William M. Chase and Robert Henri. Speicher's expressive, simplified figures owe something to Cézanne, whose work the two young painters also discovered in the library at this time.[7] Cézanne's paintings were considered to be "subversive stuff" at the institute according to Schucker, who also recalls that the single teacher who had any background in cubism was fired because of it before Louis and his friend even got to know him.[8] Abstract art as such simply "didn't exist" at the school, the atmosphere of which was so restricted that in Schucker's view the primary problem he and Louis faced was "to develop as artists in any sense of the word."

In addition to library visits, the two friends also visited museums in Baltimore and Washington together. Schucker does not specifically recall visits to the National Gallery or Phillips Collection, although he thinks such events likely, but he does recall their studying the paintings by James A. M. Whistler at the Freer Gallery. Even more clear in his memory, however, are the two or three visits that he and Louis made to the Cone Collection at times when the apartments were opened to Maryland Institute students. Since Schucker remembers that Dr. Claribel had already died, these visits must have taken place between 1930 and 1932.

It was readily apparent to the two men that Etta Cone was concentrating on Matisse's work, for new examples could be seen after each of her European trips. As Schucker describes Miss Cone and these visits,

Morris and I always went together. She would walk around with us from one end of the apartment to the other. She would talk about the artist and talk about the work. By that time we were very knowledgeable, maybe not verbally, but knowledgeable in sensibility. We could see what was there and really appreciate it. She never asked about our work, never saw anything we did. She liked us as people but that was the limit to it. [9]

When their studies at the institute were concluded Schucker won a scholarship to study in Europe in a competition judged by Roland J. McKinney, then director of the Baltimore Museum. [10] Louis apparently had not the slightest chance of winning, for McKinney "couldn't see Louis's work at all," according to Schucker. When he returned from Europe in 1933 the friendship with Louis was renewed and the two fledgling artists rented studios in a downtown office building. To support himself during these difficult years, Louis took a variety of menial jobs: peeling vegetables for an Italian restaurant, wrapping clothes in a laundry, gathering information for the Gallup Poll, and mowing grass in a cemetery (until blisters forced him to quit).

Both Louis and Schucker, like so many artists of the period, faced a crisis in their art that was a direct outgrowth of the country's financial crisis. As Schucker recalls, "It struck both of us that there was nowhere to go and nothing to do. We couldn't earn anything. We began to question a lot of what we'd done before and both tried to paint landscapes from nature [on the shore overlooking the Chesapeake Bay] as well as things in the studio." Despite the hardships they endured neither artist would give up the resolve that had developed during the years at the Maryland Institute. "We decided absolutely and desperately that we both wanted the whole thing," says Schucker, in recalling their uncompromising intention to succeed on their own terms.

This very attitude provided the fuel that propelled so many artists into the federally sponsored art projects, the earliest of which was the Emergency Work (later Relief) Bureau initiated by the College Art Association in New York in December 1932. The most effective of these programs was the Federal Art Project of the Works Progress (later Projects) Administration (WPA), which was officially authorized in October 1935 and expired in June 1943. Both Louis and Schucker took advantage of government support, initially by assisting on mural projects in Baltimore in 1934. Soon thereafter Schucker went to a Civilian Conservation Corps camp in Virginia; when he returned to Baltimore a year later he learned that Louis had moved to New York. Schucker himself soon moved to Chicago, where he joined the Easel Project of the WPA, and later moved to New York, where he still lives. He and Louis were never again as close as they had been, but they remained in contact until Louis's death.

Although Schucker was unable to recall any details about either his or Louis's Baltimore mural project, fortunate circumstances have brought to light Louis's mural and the details regarding its commission. The extant mural was recently rediscovered in the Hampstead Hill School by Mildred Blum, a docent at the Baltimore Museum of Art, who passed the information on to me. [11] The mural bears the date June 1934 and the signatures of Sam Swerdloff, Calvin Hisley, and Maurice Bernstein. Now located in New York, Swerdloff has kindly offered his recollections of the project. It was actually he who received the commission and then was assigned Hisley and Bernstein as assistants; he has confirmed that "Maurice" Bernstein was the same artist who later changed his name to Morris Louis, a fact further confirmed by a listing in the 1934 *Report of the Public Works of Art Project*. [12]

Swerdloff received the commission in January 1934 from the Public Works of Art Project (PWAP). Neither Swerdloff nor his two assistants had any

Detail, lower left, panel 3 of *History of the Written Word* showing date and names of muralists Sam Swerdloff, Calvin Hisley, and Maurice Bernstein [Morris Louis]. Hampstead Hill School, Baltimore, Maryland.

previous experience in painting, a situation characteristic of most artists in the 1930s. As Swerdloff recalls, Louis did not particularly enjoy the mural work, but the pay was considered excellent. According to his federal payroll record, Louis received $26.50 per week, the minimum paid by the PWAP, but Swerdloff was likely paid the maximum of $42.50 since he directed the commission.

The PWAP had been founded late in 1933, beginning under an emergency mandate for the winter with expiration scheduled for February 1934 and later extended to April. In June it was officially ended, having employed 3,749 artists nationwide in projects intended to decorate nonfederal public buildings and parks. As Francis V. O'Connor has explained, a dual standard was used to select artists: "First, the artist had actually to be in need of employment, and, second, he had to be qualified to produce work which would constitute a genuine embellishment of public property."[13] The potential and actual conflicts between the issues of economic relief and artistic quality haunted the PWAP and all subsequent government art projects. Subject matter was to reflect "the American scene in all its phases," according to Edward Bruce, the director of the PWAP: in New York this was interpreted loosely enough to permit a few artists working in abstract and semiabstract styles to participate, including Burgoyne Diller.

The subject matter of the mural on which Louis assisted Swerdloff was "The History of the Written Word," a theme appropriate for the school library in which it occupied three five-by-twenty-foot canvas panels installed about ten feet above the floor between the tops of bookcases and the ceiling. All three panels were executed in situ, a working condition that severely taxed the inexperienced muralists.[14] As was so often the case with federal mural projects in the 1930s, the most important artistic model for Swerdloff and his assistants was the example of the Mexican muralists José Clemente Orozco, David Alfaro Siqueiros, and Diego Rivera, whose American commissions had received widespread publicity. Echoes of the Mexicans' style of simplified figures conceived in linear terms appeared in the first sketches for the Baltimore project and are clearly evident in the murals themselves. These sketches and some preparatory drawings had to be worked up with only one week's notice, according to Swerdloff. They were sent to Washington for submission to the "National Exhibition of Art by the Public Works of Art Project," which was held at the Corcoran Gallery of Art in April and May 1934.[15] All three men worked on the studies, now presumed lost, and on each of the three painted panels.

Panel 1, *History of the Written Word.*

Detail of panel 1, center right.

The murals have survived in excellent condition, probably as a result of the high quality of the canvas and handground pigments, which were applied very thinly. The first panel depicts the development of written language; it includes cavemen drawing, Egyptian scribes, a rabbi holding the Torah, a Roman reading engraved tablets, and a Christian monk working on a manuscript. Louis's most significant contributions to the project were his research on early forms of writing and his devising a method of stylization for the basic forms used on the painted panel. This aspect of his participation becomes particularly interesting in the light of some paintings and drawings he executed in the early 1950s that indicate his renewed interest in symbolic forms of writing. These later works also reflect Louis's interest in a similar direction explored in the 1940s by several abstract expressionists, notably Jackson Pollock and Adolph Gottlieb, who used hieroglyphic forms as a means of conveying a universal content.

Louis's contribution to the execution of the other two panels was apparently more general in nature. Panel 2 depicts producers of the written word set against an English landscape with a Shakespearean theater on the left and a

Detail of panel 2, left side.

Detail of panel 2, right side.

view of the Baltimore skyline on the right. Among the writers evident are William Shakespeare, John Keats, Eugene O'Neill, Walt Whitman, Edgar Allan Poe, and Ralph Waldo Emerson. Among the actors and fictional characters depicted are Paul Robeson as Emperor Jones and John Barrymore as Hamlet. Panel 3 illustrates the modern production of books; Swerdloff used Louis as the model for one of the illustrators (see details of panel 3, left side). The panel concludes with a scene of a librarian giving books to students, an obvious reference to the mural's setting. Louis worked with Swerdloff from January until mid-April, after which the latter brought the project to completion without assistance.

Panel 3, *History of the Written Word.*

When the PWAP ended, artists in Baltimore, New York, Chicago, and other major cities began to organize branches of the Artists' Union. Its major national goals were the protection of artists' rights and the institution of a permanent, federally sponsored art project. The burgeoning labor movement served as an important model for the artists' groups, some of which were inspired by the labor groups to use similarly volatile tactics. Early members of the Baltimore Artists' Union included Sam Swerdloff, Chet LaMore, Mervin Jules, Herman Maril, and Morris Louis. In addition the membership included the artist wives of several important local businessmen; as a result of these latter participants the Baltimore group assumed a totally nonmilitant posture.[16] One of its main goals was to pressure the Baltimore Museum and Roland McKinney into exhibiting the work of living artists, a goal that was

Detail of panel 3, left side.

eventually achieved. Mervin Jules, who had previously been involved with the New York Artists' Union when he was a student at the Art Students League, was elected president of the Baltimore group in 1934. When he decided to return to New York in 1935, Morris Louis assumed the presidency. (When Louis was applying for a job at the University of Maryland in 1952, he mentioned in his correspondence and on the accompanying résumé that he had been president in 1935 of the "Baltimore Artists' Association." This alteration to a more neutral term possibly reflects his desire, during the period of Senator Joseph McCarthy's power, to avoid possible questions as to his youthful communist sympathies, which were assumed by McCarthy—with good justification—to go hand in hand with some union memberships in the 1930s.)[17]

Louis soon followed the example of Mervin Jules and moved to New York, apparently in 1936. Since he had little money and no place to stay he turned to Chet LaMore, one of his Baltimorean acquaintances who had also already settled in the city.[18] LaMore has recalled, "I offered to let him bunk in our loft on West 21st Street and he agreed to paint the loft floor in return." LaMore's recollections of Louis during his month-long stay are valuable, for they offer a unique glimpse of him during this most difficult period.

He came and slept. Every morning he had breakfast at the cafeteria on 23rd and 7th. After that every morning *he walked across town to the Japan Paper Co. (which was on 30th or 31st between Madison and Park)* and bought 1 ONE *sheet of good drawing paper with which he returned to the loft —sat down and did* a drawing, *line only. As I remember the drawings they were satirical figure subject matter — interesting and good. That accomplished without any but minimal verbal utterance —he would get out the gallon can of dark red paint, arrange my low rocking chair parallel to the edge of yesterday's painted area —dip the brush in the can and gently rock his way along. He only bent his arm when it was necessary to reload the brush with paint. I am not sure if he ever finished the floor —it didn't seem important even to me by that time —at any rate —he found a girl and promptly arranged for new quarters and a better lifestyle. And that is all I can tell you except to add that he struck me as being very reserved —non-communicative —to the degree which suggests "withdrawn," but it is not my province to dabble in such definitions.* [19]

Louis's improved lifestyle may have been a result of a part-time job he obtained as a window decorator, making models out of straw, which supplemented the small allowance he received from his family as well as the packages of food and painting materials they sent him. Mervin Jules recalls that Louis's daily food allowance of twenty-five cents was more often spent for cigarettes than for food. Louis also was one of many artists who took advantage of the generosity of the paint manufacturer Leonard Bocour, who ran a small shop on West Fifteenth Street. Bocour initiated what he termed the "Bocour bread line," an arrangement by which he gave away small waxed paper packages of the paint that was left over after he had filled the tubes for a given batch of color, an operation then accomplished by hand. Louis visited the shop two or three times a week to pick up these free paint supplies. [20]

Louis's résumé stated that during the period he spent in New York he participated in a "workshop with a group of artists —Siqueiros and others — in experimental forms and Duco techniques." The Siqueiros Workshop opened on West Fourteenth Street in April 1936 and "gradually disintegrated after Siqueiros' departure for Spain in early 1937." [21] Its most famous American participant was Jackson Pollock, but other members included Axel Horn and Mervin Jules, who shared a loft where Siqueiros often stayed since it was located near the workshop. The group activities involved experiments with new tools, materials, and techniques, including "methods of working collectively." [22] Just as Pollock's innovations in painting may owe something to this experience so, too, Louis's paintings after 1953 may stem partially from this venture, recollections of which his oft-cited visit to Helen Frankenthaler's studio in 1953 might have stimulated. "Collective painting," for example, is precisely what Louis and Noland practiced immediately after that visit, although Noland termed it "jam painting." [23]

Equally if not more important than the technical experiments at the workshop was its political goal of creating "art for the people," in the form of floats and posters for such political events as the May Day parade and antifascist rallies, as well as specific projects commissioned by the American Communist Party. Participation in the workshop did not necessarily imply party membership, but certainly reflected strong sympathies in that direction. According to the recollections of his friends during this period, Louis shared with most artists and intellectuals of the 1930s a commitment to leftist causes. He probably participated in the marches and demonstrations organized by the Artists' Union and publicized in *Art Front,* the organization's house organ.

In February 1937 Louis was one of a small group of Baltimorean painters, including Mervin Jules and Herman Maril, who exhibited together at the ACA Gallery on Eighth Street. Like the majority of works displayed there, many of the paintings in this exhibition depicted subjects with markedly socialist overtones. As Joseph Solman reported in a review in *Art Front,* "Morris Louis contributes *Evicted* and *Talk of Relief,* paintings handled in the key of the Mexicans." [24] This first known mention in print of Louis's work and the first public indication that he had changed his name make it clear that he had adopted the social-realist subject matter characteristic of so much painting in

New York during the 1930s. Furthermore, his experience with the PWAP and the Siqueiros Workshop had also inspired him to work in the style of the Mexicans.

Late in October 1938 Louis applied for a second Social Security number under his recently adopted name. He listed as his address 1362 Sixth Avenue, although later correspondence with his family indicates that he had moved to 334 East Twenty-fourth Street by October 1941. His new Social Security card designated him "unemployed as of 10-27-38"; apparently not too long afterwards he applied to the WPA and was put on the Easel Division of the Federal Art Project. Federal payroll records indicate that Louis was employed by the WPA from February 27, 1939, until August 27, 1940, at a salary of $91.10 per month.

Like all other artists on the WPA, Louis would have had to qualify first for home relief after a stringent investigation proved that he was destitute. Only then was he eligible for the WPA salary, which he would have collected in person each week. Since the young woman with whom he lived at this time was an art teacher also employed by the WPA, their combined incomes would have permitted them to live rather well according to the standards of the time. (The WPA doubtlessly caused many marriages between artists to be postponed because one of the salaries would have been canceled in the event of a marriage.) Louis must have enjoyed the relative freedom that made the Easel Project so favored by artists who worked in their own studios and brought finished work to their supervisors.[25] According to schedules established by Holger Cahill, in 1939 an artist on the Easel Project was expected to work 130 hours per month and to complete, for example, an oil painting sixteen by twenty inches or twenty by twenty-four inches, or two watercolors or gouaches during that period. This relatively unstructured system replaced an earlier policy that had required every artist to sign in at a central office every morning, a system both time wasting and ineffectual.[26]

Louis would have been forced to accustom himself to the nagging uncertainties resulting from constant threat of cutbacks that plagued the WPA artists and reduced the employment rolls by more than half between 1936 and September 1939. When administration of the New York project was shifted from Washington to local control in July 1939, the emphasis was shifted away from individual artists and toward the Community Art Centers. Under the direction of Colonel Brehon Somervell an eighteen-month rule was instituted in August 1939; it required dismissal and recertification of any artist who had been on the rolls for eighteen months or more. Employment dropped by seventy percent as a result. Louis left the project precisely eighteen months after he joined; according to his WPA record, he resigned, having found "outside employment."

He remained in New York, however, at least through 1941 since letters to his eldest brother from October and December of that year testify to his continued residence in the city. The earlier of the two letters provides some insight into Louis's attitude toward the art world after nearly six years in its midst. He wrote:

As to the painting, I know that I'd have had a gallery long ago had it been in me to popularize my style. However, that is not the case, and so I have to play for big stakes in hopes that some highly reputable joint will handle the stuff some day. They might sell such stuff whereas it is out of the question for a minor gallery to do so.

Had I been interested in medicine, for instance, I would go in for research, new fields, etc. That is the kind of make-up I have and it would not be good for me to try to change. I'm willing to gamble that some day I'll be in a big spot. As long as I can keep going I don't mind taking in a movie every 2 weeks instead of weekly. It is a small sacrifice and I assure you that I'm eating plenty and feeling fine. I really have suffered nothing by staying in NY and have gained a feeling that I'm on my own, which is important. [27]

Exactly how much longer he was able to remain on his own in New York is uncertain. His résumé states that he returned to Baltimore in 1940, which is clearly inaccurate, but both his widow and Leonard Bocour recall that he returned about 1944 or '45. He was never drafted into military service and was apparently classified "4 F." He moved back into his parents' home, relied on financial support from his brothers, the youngest of whom he assisted in a small pharmaceutical business, and used the basement of the house for his studio. All of these conditions and the resulting loss of independence left him dejected and depressed; his widow — then his next-door neighbor — recalls seeing him slouched on a porch chair, a brooding and frustrated man. Louis would have to wait thirteen more years from the date of his letter of October 1941 until a "highly reputable joint," the Kootz Gallery, showed three of his paintings in 1954 in an "Emerging Talent" exhibition selected by Clement Greenberg. No matter how grateful he may have been for that opportunity, Louis must also have felt bitter about having had to endure such a long wait from that time, some twenty years earlier, when he and Charles Schucker decided "absolutely and desperately" that they wanted the "whole thing."

PAINTINGS AND DRAWINGS, 1930–1945

Although knowledge of Louis's early career is still somewhat fragmentary, enough dated works are available (either in the original or in photographs) to make possible the placement of the few drawings and gouaches dated earlier than 1945 in a context that clarifies Louis's level of achievement during that period. A quick scanning of the work provides clear justification for the attitude toward Louis shared by his artist friends in the 1930s. The seriousness of his intentions and commitment was widely acknowledged, but he was perceived to be a poor draftsman who had no promise. [28]

One of his earliest extant works is drawing #504, a portrait of Stephens Berge, an acquaintance and fellow student at the Maryland Institute of Art. This fact would suggest a date of about 1930, but since Louis signed the drawing "Maurice," an invented name used elsewhere only on the 1934 PWAP mural, the Berge drawing was probably done at about the same time as the mural. Mr. Berge recalls that Louis's lack of money prompted Berge and his brother, also an artist, to permit Louis to use their studio and to share models a few times. Although Berge sat for this drawing, he has remarked, "It was not a likeness, but he wasn't interested in likenesses." [29]

Despite Mr. Berge's recollection, the resulting drawing does project a degree of specificity, notably in the contour of the face and chin, where Louis worked

Portrait of Stephens Berge, drawing #504, circa 1930–34. The Maryland Institute, College of Art, Baltimore.

Unless otherwise indicated, the works are from The Estate of Morris Louis. The method used to number and date the drawings is described on pages 69–73 of the Catalogue, which is fully illustrated.

with particular care to achieve a satisfactory line. Light, tentative lines were later clarified by darker, more assured ones. The facial features were also conceived carefully, so much so that the sitter's pensive expression comes to appear fixed. Louis allowed himself greater freedom in rendering the hair, rapidly sketching it with short, delicate lines and refraining from establishing clear contours. His technique focuses attention on the face, suggests highlights, and also counters the slight sense of three dimensionality established by the value variation of the lines. Similarly, the rendering of the shirt creates a surface pattern rather than volume.

The extent to which the Berge drawing was intended to be a portrait, whether or not Louis was able to realize his goal, is more obvious when the drawing is compared to a gouache entitled *Young Man in the City*, dated 1937 and signed "M. Louis," the first known signature that reflects his nom de plume. The gouache is extremely dark in tonality and depicts a male head and shoulders centered on the page and viewed frontally at very close range. Skyscrapers rise like two enclosing pillars and a small wedge of sky appears to rest on the head like a crown. Because of the date and subject matter it is likely that the gouache was done after Louis arrived in New York and that the artist himself is the young man. Unlike the Berge drawing, facial features are here generalized and the head rendered as a regular oval that emphasizes its iconic quality. The expressionist aspects of color and form seem to owe much to Marsden Hartley and also to reflect a mode explored in contemporary work by the New York group that called itself "The Ten" and included Mark Rothko and Adolph Gottlieb among its members.

In 1939 Louis executed a chalk portrait of a woman (D498B), possibly the young artist with whom he lived after he left Chet LaMore's loft. (Louis's financial need during this period is further confirmed by the fact that in 1940 he used the other side of this paper for a gouache landscape, D498A.) He was

Young Man in the City, 1937, gouache on paper, dimensions unknown. Location unknown.

Drawing D498B, 1939.

Pablo Picasso, *Woman with a Helmet of Hair,* 1904, gouache, 16¼ x 11¾ inches. The Art Institute of Chicago, Illinois.

evidently inspired by Pablo Picasso's Blue Period portraits of about 1904, perhaps feeling a particular affinity for them since they were done at a time when Picasso's situation closely resembled Louis's in 1939. As an artist in his mid-twenties who had left a provincial home for a major art capital in which he had learned to endure poverty and enjoy the companionship of a young woman, Louis, like Picasso before him, used formal simplifications and a somber tonality to capture his sitter's gaunt features and dejected mood. Louis's achievement is obviously no match for Picasso's, but he does seem to have tried to respond to work that he could easily have seen in the Picasso retrospective that Alfred Barr organized for the Museum of Modern Art in 1939. One of the Blue Period works in that exhibition was the gouache *Woman with a Helmet of Hair* (1904), the subject of which has an upswept pompadour crowning her face in a manner quite similar to the hairstyle in Louis's portrait.

Untitled, circa 1937, oil on canvas, dimensions unknown. Location unknown.

With a technique similar to that evident in the Berge drawing, Louis worked in a loose, abbreviated manner to block in the woman's shoulder area without attempting to endow the figure with three-dimensional substance. Her hair is also rendered more suggestively than descriptively; black and brown looping lines accent the area and distinguish it from the face and neck, which are shaded with the same crayon tones. Finally Louis used green chalk to outline the ear, shade the nose, and sign the drawing.

The two paintings that Louis exhibited at the ACA Gallery in 1937 are presumed lost, but a few extant oil paintings and gouaches from the period demonstrate his interest in social-realist subjects and the manner of working "in the key of the Mexicans" that Joseph Solman observed. One untitled oil painting, acquired from the artist in 1937, depicts a man seated in the foreground with three smaller figures in the background walking in front of a

Untitled, circa 1937, oil on canvas, dimensions unknown. Location unknown.

massive, stepped wall that blocks a view into the distance. The barren urban setting, like the figures, is rendered in browns, grays, and black. The bulky male figure conveys the tone of defeat and impassivity so commonly depicted in subjects of the depression period. This image, as well as the titles of the pictures recorded in Solman's review, indicates that Louis did not avoid the grim aspects of New York during the 1930s. Similarly, another untitled oil painting of this period depicts a man lying on his back on a city street, clutching a pint bottle of alcohol in one hand and a smoking pistol in the other. The bloody wound on his forehead provides the evidence of his recent suicide. This melodrama is heightened by the surreal image in the sky of two framed images of women, possibly photographs of the victim's wife and mother, who serve as reminders of his inability to confront his family in the face of his own failure.

Drawing D497 [1938–40].

Not all of Louis's extant works from this period are similarly dismal. The compressed space, primitive rendering of figures, loose technique, and striking contrast of complementary colors of the gouache D497 appear to reflect his interest in such expressionists as Ernst Kirchner or Emil Nolde, as does a subject that may well be a brothel scene. Louis drew this image in pencil before applying the colors in gouache and then used black paint to clarify — in a crude manner — the basic contours of the figures. A second gouache, D502, probably from about the same time, uses more subdued hues and a dense patterning that collapses the space and imparts energy to a scene of two waiters carrying trays across the tiled floor of a restaurant.

Charles Schucker remarked that he and Louis had turned to landscape painting at a time when they questioned the validity of their previous work. Louis again tried his hand at landscapes about 1939 when he traveled to New

Drawing D502 [1938–40].

England to visit a sister-in-law. One resulting oil painting, *Broken Bridge* (ca. 1939) was apparently exhibited at the 1939 New York World's Fair.[30] The picture shares with an untitled gouache (D498A) from 1940 and a few other landscapes of the same period restriction of space related to that observed in the urban scenes discussed above. The bridge in D498A is particularly flattened, its dark shape standing out in sharp relief against the water; it resembles an anthropomorphic, mechanical figure that appears to support the distant hills. In a rather crude interpretation of Cézanne's landscape space, perhaps absorbed from Marsden Hartley's landscapes of about 1909, Louis creates a scene that rises up the picture plane in horizontal layers.

The comparison with Hartley is more striking in the case of drawing D498A,

Broken Bridge, circa 1939, oil on canvas, 26¹/₁₆ x 30¹/₈ inches.

Drawing D498A, 1940.

Marsden Hartley, *The Dark Mountain No. 2,* 1909, oil on composition board, 20 x 24 inches. The Metropolitan Museum of Art, New York; the Alfred Stieglitz Collection, 1949.

in which the towering mass of the mountain entirely closes off the spatial recession and contributes to an oppressive, brooding scene quite similar to that in Hartley's *The Dark Mountain No. 2* (1909), one of a group of pictures characterized by Alfred Stieglitz as the artist's "dark mountain period."[31] Louis's landscapes are also generally dark and melancholy, with massive mountains that leave only a narrow margin of sky with a hovering moon or sun. The picket fence featured so prominently in D498A is common in Louis's landscapes of the period. An acquaintance of Louis's in the early 1950s reported that picket fences continued to interest him, although at that time he was working in a more abstract manner, trying to capture the shadow cast by such a fence.[32]

Two additional gouaches, D495 and D503, date from about the same period, but they display an agitated, even frenzied energy not evident in the other paintings. Both appear to depict one or two figures in rowboats, but the freedom Louis exercised with regard to drawing, color, and space prevents a

Drawing D495 [1940–45].

Drawing D503 [1940–45].

more precise identification. The boldness of color is most unusual in his early work as is the thickness of the paint caused by the brushing of light values and bright hues over underlying colors. It is possible that Louis was influenced by the dynamic energies of John Marin's watercolors of the Maine coast, although the compressed space of Louis's work is notably different from Marin's effective use of unpainted areas to infuse his subjects with light. Similarly, although D495 employs the framing device so characteristic of Marin's work, it is here rendered in dense, vivid colors rather than as a margin of breathing space. Nonetheless, Louis's willingness to develop the expressionistic potential of his previous work and to sacrifice his prior commitment to a more careful rendering of nature signal a maturation in his work.

It is likely that these works bear witness to the cumulative experience of his first years in New York when he was able for the first time to see modern American and European art in museums and galleries. The work examined thus far does not demonstrate an unusual talent or a remarkably rapid assimilation of avant-garde ideas. In fact, quite the contrary, for the social-realist paintings reveal Louis's interest in pursuing — or at least his willingness to pursue — a style and subject matter that was widespread at the time; in other words, he did "popularize" his style, despite his claim in 1941 to the contrary. Apparently the early 1940s marked a change in his approach, however — a fact which makes it particularly unfortunate that so few works from that period have survived.

Louis's receptivity to modern trends evidently continued to expand. By 1948, the first year from which a large number of drawings have survived, he focused his attention seriously on Pablo Picasso, Henri Matisse, and Joan Miró, and soon also upon some of his own contemporaries, notably Jackson Pollock and Arshile Gorky. These drawings represent the first aesthetically significant body of his extant oeuvre and in them, for the first time, we can perceive an emerging sense of confidence and the attainment of original achievement.

THE MIDDLE YEARS, 1947–1953

The great majority of Louis's drawings date not from his early years but from the next period in his life. In retrospect, these years from 1947 through 1953 constitute a bridge between his experiences as a young artist struggling both to survive and to find a viable direction for his work, and the final eight years of his life, which were characterized by major innovative painting and, eventually, by the beginnings of public recognition. The last period of his career has provided the focus for all previous examinations of Louis's work and will not be further discussed, since no extant drawings date from those years, nor is there any evidence to suggest that Louis made drawings after 1953. Instead, the focus here will be concentrated on Louis's middle years, a period just as long — or as short, depending upon one's perspective — as his artistic maturity. Between 1947 and 1953 he absorbed important lessons from vanguard art until its potentials for him were exhausted; only after this clearly synthetic interval was he prepared to carve out a new territory, one uniquely his own.

In terms of Louis's life experiences the period begins with his marriage to Marcella Siegel in July 1947 and resulting departure from Baltimore for Silver Spring, Maryland, a suburb of Washington, D.C., where he moved into his wife's two-room apartment. They converted the bedroom into his studio and used the other room for living, eating, and sleeping. Louis's widow recalls a small gray sauce pan of rabbitskin glue sizing intermittently boiling on the stove in the cramped kitchen, which served both studio and domestic functions.

Louis's ties with Baltimore were not severed by the move, for he exhibited in the annual Maryland artists exhibitions at the Baltimore Museum from 1948 through 1950 and in 1952, and also in the Baltimore "National Watercolor Exhibition" of 1949.[33] Louis also exhibited at the city's Peale Museum in 1950 and served on the Artists' Committee of the Baltimore Museum in 1950 and in 1952, acting as the Artists' Equity representative during the second term. In addition, beginning in 1951 he commuted to the city once a week to teach a group of private students who had sought him out.[34] He also came to know Kenneth Sawyer, then the art critic for the *Baltimore Sun,* who was most receptive to his work.[35]

In 1952 Louis and his wife moved into Washington, where they had purchased a home on Legation Street, NW. Louis converted the twelve- by fourteen-foot dining room of the house into the studio that he was to use for the rest of his life. During the same year Jacob Kainen, a Washington artist, helped Louis to obtain a teaching position at the Washington Workshop Center of the Arts, founded by Leon and Ida Berkowitz in 1945. Louis taught adult painting classes two evenings a week. Despite the fact that most of his students were amateurs, he took the job very seriously.[36] In 1953 Louis obtained a teaching position for one term at Howard University and, at about the same time, began to teach private pupils in Washington in addition to his group in Baltimore.

At the Washington Workshop Louis met Kenneth Noland, who became his closest friend at this time. It was through Noland that Louis met Clement Greenberg, whose support and encouragement proved so central to Louis's eventual widespread recognition. Noland has described his friendship with Louis as follows:

Morris Louis (left) teaching at the Workshop Center of the Arts. *Washington Post,* March 13, 1953.

I knew a lot of other artists but I really became a close friend of Morris' mostly because our interests in art coincided. I felt an affinity with his preferences in art more than I did with most other artists in Washington that I knew. So we became painting buddies . . . we'd see each other, oh, two or three times a week and we talked a lot. We were very close friends for about the first two years that we knew each other . . . he was very interested in Jackson Pollock, and so was I . . . he had arrived at this independently. I had arrived at it mostly through having had contact with Clement Greenberg. There was idealism, personal idealism . . . involved in that. . . . We were checking and comparing and bringing other kinds of information to each other —for instance we both liked Bob Motherwell's work.[37]

Louis was not particularly friendly with other Washington artists at that time or later in his career. As Gene Davis recalls:

I met Morris Louis at the Washington Workshop for the Arts in 1953, I think. I can remember Leon Berkowitz introducing me to him. He was standing up on a ladder painting the ceiling of Ida's office. He reached down, shook hands with me, and that was the last time I saw him for about five years. He was rather a recluse and didn't mingle too much. I think I saw him only three times in my life, despite the fact that we were Washingtonians and he was in the art world.[38]

Although Washington's "art scene" during the years under consideration was measurably livelier than the one Louis had encountered in Baltimore, aside from his teaching Louis apparently participated very little in it. The National Gallery and the Phillips Collection offered a wealth of rich visual material; Louis surely visited both collections, but it is difficult to determine how directly he was influenced by their contents.[39] The Watkins Gallery at American University and the biennials at the Corcoran Gallery brought to Washington works by a wide range of artists from across the country that Louis may well have seen.

Even more important for local artists than the established museums were the Institute of Contemporary Art, founded in 1947 under the directorship of Robert Richman, and the Workshop Center of the Arts, both of which sponsored exhibitions and classes. The ICA also initiated a lecture series that brought to Washington such distinguished speakers as Stanley William Hayter, Naum Gabo, Josef Albers, W. H. Auden, e. e. cummings, T. S. Eliot, and Edith Sitwell. Since the lectures were generally held in the evenings, however, it is unlikely that Louis attended. He was an early riser whose day often began as early as five o'clock in the morning, and as a result he was usually too tired to go out in the evening. For other artists in the city, the activities of these two centers provided a stimulating environment that Barbara Rose has deemed comparable to the Artists' Club in New York.

Despite his reclusive habits Louis gradually began to be better known after 1952. In February 1953 his work was included in a staff exhibition at the Washington Workshop Center that marked the second term of the school. Louis and Noland were singled out in a *Washington Post* review as "young artists [who] have attained a considerable maturity in the handling of pigment and in the technical control of a difficult idiom." Louis's affinities with Pollock were noted and his compositions were described as "well organized spatially, with a strong feeling for the third dimension."[40]

Just two months later the workshop gave Louis his first one-man exhibition. He showed thirteen painting from 1951 and 1952, three collages dated 1952–53, and "selected drawings" from 1953, the only drawings exhibited during his lifetime and apparently the work on which his energies had been concentrated during this period. Leon Berkowitz noted in his introduction to the catalogue the personal, organic calligraphy that characterized the paintings. He cited comparisons with Joan Miró, Paul Klee, Salvador Dali, and Max Ernst, but perceived an originality in Louis's work that transcended those possible influences. The *Washington Post*'s favorable and lengthy review noted that the work of the "young newcomer from Baltimore" demonstrated a "strong cohesion, whether the forms are nebulous and free, or whether an architectural structure binds them in severely controlled geometries."[41] In a similar vein the critic for the *Times-Herald* observed that Louis "promises a plastic emotional understanding that is as cohesive and sincere as it is personally decorative and free."[42]

This first one-man exhibition in April 1953 marks the conclusion of Louis's "middle years." It was during the same month that Louis joined Noland for a weekend in New York where they met and saw the work of Franz Kline and Helen Frankenthaler. The two Washington artists were excited and challenged by the experience; when they returned home they worked together for a while, "jam painting like jazz," in Noland's term, in an effort "to break down their previous assumptions about painting."[43] Louis was apparently so intent upon developing his painting after this experience that drawing per se ceased to be an issue for him, although it is obvious that part of the achievement of his subsequent paintings derives from the draftsmanship inherent in the contours of poured color areas.

After 1953 his career was marked by an increasingly public profile. Beginning with the "Emerging Talent" exhibition that Greenberg selected in 1954 for the Kootz Gallery, Louis's work was shown in New York and, after 1960, also in Europe. His exhibitions were reviewed regularly, if not always positively. Greenberg's essay "Louis and Noland," which appeared in the May

1960 issue of *Art International*, generated widespread interest in the work, particularly since the influential critic had not written so positively about relatively unknown artists for a number of years. Louis did not live long enough to enjoy the acclaim that now greets his mature paintings, but after 1953 he was no longer forced to endure the obscurity that had characterized the first twenty years of his career.

DRAWINGS, 1947–1953

Many of Louis's drawings date from just two or three years, 1948–49 and 1953, rather than being dispersed evenly throughout the two decades from the mid-thirties to the mid-fifties that witnessed his interest in the medium. This pattern is probably as much or more a reflection of his financial situation during those few years than it is an indication of his desire to tackle the issues of draftsmanship. This conclusion is suggested by his widow's recollection

Drawing D78 [1948].

that Louis turned to drawing when he had no money for painting supplies or when supplies that had been ordered failed to arrive on time. Although his wife's income provided regular support after their marriage — with the exception of a period in 1953 when she was between jobs — there was not enough money for Louis to buy paint or canvas in large quantities until 1960, when he began to sell some paintings. Since he ordered both paint and canvas from New York, a shipping delay usually forced him temporarily to stop working for total lack of supplies. In the first years of the marriage he also had more time for his art since he was no longer working for his brother; by 1953, however, he was teaching two groups of private students as well as his classes at the Washington Workshop.

In addition to financial pressures, one other practical situation prompted Louis to concentrate for short periods of time on drawing in lieu of painting. These were the nearly annual trips that he and his wife made to visit his parents and brothers after they relocated in Florida in 1947. Physically separated from his studio for about a week during these winter trips, Louis turned to drawing as the most convenient way to work. The results of at least one of these trips will be examined later, but one point should be stressed from the outset: regardless of Louis's apparent disdain for the medium of drawing as against that of painting, many of his drawings are wonderfully relaxed and joyous, while others are so rich and complex that they indicate his serious regard for them. It is obvious that Louis could become fully engrossed in a drawing and derive much pleasure from it.

Despite the fact that so many drawings date from 1948–49, no single example or group emerges as the obvious chronological introduction to the group as a whole nor is a clear stylistic evolution evident. D78 and D94, two drawings that share a related subject but present a dramatic contrast in overall conception will, however, provide an enlightening prelude. The first, D78, is a male head, one of a group of eight similar drawings all apparently executed in the late 1940s. Since several of this group were found in notebooks purchased in Florida, it is possible that family members were the general inspiration. Louis's widow has cautioned, however, that formal portrait sittings were totally uncharacteristic of Louis's practice.

Matisse's draftsmanship is one likely inspiration for the fluid contour that describes these heads. The tentativeness of the Berge portrait has given way to a more assured handling of the pen, which often captures the shape of the head and the facial features in a few strokes. The same basic schema served Louis in all eight drawings, the differences of which arise primarily from variations in the head shapes. Similar in many respects to the *Young Man in the City* (see p. 23) these iconic heads do not achieve the sense of personality and psychological probity projected by, for example, Matisse's self-portrait drawings of 1945, although the means employed by the two artists are related. Louis's heads are not entirely lacking in character, for the expressions range from a rather withdrawn or wary evasiveness to a direct, almost naïve engagement with the spectator.

The second work that completes this prelude, D94, also depicts a head. But in this instance, calm, iconic stasis is abandoned in favor of a marvelously ferocious image replete with fangs and scrambled facial features wildly suggested by loops and spirals. Even the background participates in the visual uproar, for jagged spirals, restrained only slightly by their placement in

Henri Matisse, *Self-Portrait*, 1945, crayon on paper, 16 x 20¾ inches. The Museum of Modern Art, New York; John S. Newberry Fund.

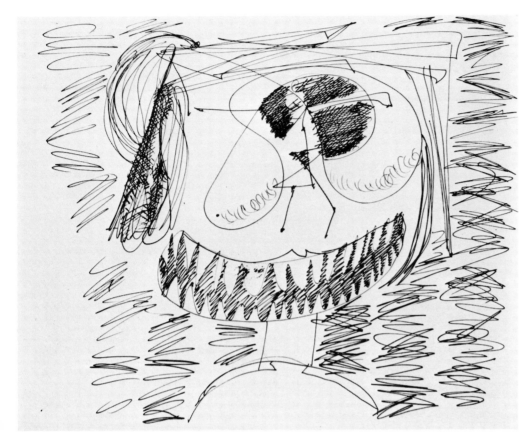

Drawing D94 [1948].

vertical channels, nearly fill the page. If Matisse lurked in Louis's mind when he conceived the previous image, then Miró or Picasso are closer in spirit here, both in terms of radical formal distortions and in the sense of humor that verges on the menacing.

Despite the apparent chasm that separates the conceptual qualities of these drawings, they share a certain touch and consistency in the handling of the pen. And not surprisingly, for they come from the same sketchpad and were probably done at about the same time. Their differences in emotional tone — the one a calm, simplifying, and generalizing approach to reality, the other an intense, extreme, and imaginative one — are features that reemerge consistently in Louis's drawings. One hesitates to invoke the much-abused terms classic and romantic, or Apollonian and Dionysian, but the polarities those words convey are evident here. This pair of drawings suggests that Louis was — consciously or not — testing the limits of his imaginative process. Certainly one significant aspect of his drawings as a whole is that they reflect a testing process in which he experimented with ideas borrowed from other artists and with his own inventions, with the stark clarity of contour drawing and the evocative richness of dense hatching, with figuration and with abstraction and, like so many of his contemporaries, with the manifold possibilities suggested by merging these last two categories. This is the wealth of material we shall now explore.

FIGURATIVE DRAWINGS, CIRCA 1948

Drawing #505, 1948. Private collection.

In 1948 Louis gave a drawing to a friend who recalls that the subject was the Budapest String Quartet, one of whose performances Louis had attended. This drawing (#505), which is both signed and dated, is very similar to four others that must have been done about the same time. If the friend's recollection is accurate, Louis treated the subject with great freedom, for the quartet is reduced to a trio in one drawing (D115) and expanded to a quintet in another (D492). Although the space resembles that of a stage, no musical instruments appear and a sun or moon hovers in the distance. Perhaps the rubbery arms that encircle one stick figure in D492 had their origin in the pose of the quartet's cellist. All of the figures are rendered in a loose, nearly capricious contour line, but the obvious speed of execution did not deprive them of individuality in pose, dress, or expression. The high-heeled lady in D156 is particularly amusing; like many of the other figures she recalls the whimsical wire creatures made by Alexander Calder in Paris during the 1920s.

Drawing D115 [1948].

Similar in certain respects to the quartet drawings, D494, an undated work in gouache and ink, also must date from the late 1940s. Executed on the cover of a drawing tablet, it is the only "finished" drawing of several that Louis made on such covers. Others of them, including D48, D66A, and D74, were scribbled in a manner that suggests limbering-up exercises more than drawings, as does the field of D494. But in this last instance Louis also created a standing, robed figure holding a staff that resembles a human stick figure with curved arms and legs wrapped around the pole. Red, yellow, and blue gouache applied over the drawing defines the figures and separates them from the complex densities of the background. The mysterious robed figure and its totemic staff emerge from the field somewhat like the figures in Pollock's paintings — *Male and Female* (1942) or *Water Figure* (1945), for example — although Louis's iconography does not appear as complex nor does his work project the high-pitched intensity of these Pollocks.

Drawing D492 [1948].

An entire group of drawings from sketchpads number 12, 17, and 18 contains a wide variety of imaginative figurative images. Drawings D1 and D2, both signed and dated 1948, also belong to this group.[44] Common to many of these drawings is a figure with a pointed head or cap who is attired in a knee-length, billowing cape (D1, D58), a courtly ruffle and knickers (D85), or apparently in nothing at all (D88). In drawings D93 and D95, its body assumes the proportions of a Giacometti-like figure with the head reduced to a tiny ball crowned by an even smaller pointed hat. This image is always accompanied by other figures, sometimes a rather voluptuous female (D88, D89, D90, D93, D95), but more often by fantastic birds (D1, D55, D58), or biomorphic, Hans Arp-like creatures not so readily named (D57, D84, D85). It engages in one recurring gesture: holding a baton or sword, it extends the rod toward one of its companions as if to honor (D58, D59), or perhaps to threaten (D87, D93, D95). In D85 the baton can be interpreted either as a life-giving wand whose force has transformed a flattened, biomorphic puddle into a standing creature, or, conversely, as a weapon that has killed one of those Arp-like creatures and caused another to flee.

Precisely what this figure is and what its actions signify remain a mystery. Is it truly a knight or perhaps some type of magician? What initially brought it

Drawing D156 [1948].

Drawing D494 [1948–49]. Private collection.

Jackson Pollock, *Water Figure,* 1945, oil on canvas, 71¾ x 29 inches. Hirshhorn Museum and Sculpture Garden, Smithsonian Institution.

Drawing D1, 1948. Jeannette F. Kear, Chevy Chase, Maryland.

Drawing D58 [1948].

Drawing D88 [1948].

out of Louis's imagination and why was this image sufficiently intriguing to provoke as many drawings as it did? Is there — or was there ever — the intention to create a continuing narrative? It is tempting to suggest a parallel between the apparent powers of the figure and those of the artist who created this fantasy world. Obviously these drawings depart from others previously examined, for in them Louis moved away both from transcribing nature and from creating humorous linear caricatures based upon human prototypes in order to tap his imagination. In the process or, more likely, in an attempt to encourage this process, he began to utilize surrealist automatist techniques, a procedure explored by many artists in New York during the early 1940s.

One especially obvious example of the interplay in Louis's work between linear figurative imagery and more abstract automatic drawing is evident in a comparison of D54 and several pages from sketchpad number 14, most notably drawing D376. In the former Louis created from fantasy wonderfully droll centipedes with long, curving snouts. Related by an imaginative process of genetic transformation to the kneeling figure in D58, two of the centipedes in D54 convey a sense of naïve innocence, while the one in the center projects malevolence. All three were clearly drawn rapidly and with great ease, so much so that a single horizontally extended looping spiral — like a slinky toy — creates both legs and their implied movement.

The images in D376 are very similar to those in D54 but are rendered in more abstract patterns, the incipient figuration of which might be overlooked without the example of the earlier work. The looping spirals in D376 are

Drawing D85 [1948].

Drawing D54 [1948].

Drawing D376 [1950–53].

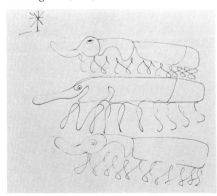

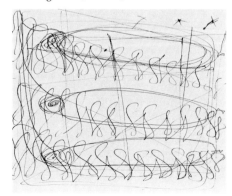

exploited almost entirely for their own sakes, although the three stars in the upper right margin provide a link to the more distinctly figurative rendering. This drawing is from sketchpad 14, the pages of which are undated, but the presence of a containing rectangle of structuring vertical lines and several ruled horizontal lines are features Louis explored in many drawings of the early 1950s. This suggests that the centipedes of D54 were probably not derived from the more automatist drawings but instead served as one of several launching pads from which Louis projected himself into nonfiguration in the early 1950s.

Pablo Picasso, *Minotauromachy*, 1935, etching, 19½ x 27⁷/₁₆ inches. The Museum of Modern Art, New York; purchase fund.

Drawing D47 [1948].

Drawing D49A [1948].

An even closer relationship between the gentle figures of the late 1940s and the more provocative surrealist vocabulary of images that Louis began deriving from automatist techniques during the same period is evident in D88 (see p. 36). Ambiguous, threatening forms are here juxtaposed to human figures, including the familiar knight. He and a dark-faced, hairy companion are confronted by a female whose aggressive posture is conveyed equally by her shape and stance. Even more menacing is the bizarre configuration in the center of the page, which can be interpreted as a huge disembodied eye and mouth or, perhaps, as a large snail and oyster shell. (The latter interpretation is suggested by comparison with a group of beach scenes discussed later.) Louis effectively employed this ambiguous form and varied, dense techniques to establish a disturbing mood, for the central images disrupt both the relationships of scale and the spatial illusion of the scene. Expanding his vocabulary from the easy, fluid contour rendering of D58 (see p. 36) to this cacophony of marks that are thick and thin, heavy and light, straight and curved, fluid and jagged, choppy and spiraling, Louis pursued a more elaborate and complex iconography. In this respect he appears to have absorbed lessons from Picasso in D88 and a number of related drawings of the same period.

The extreme density of D47, for example, and its contrast of an awesome bull or minotaur head in the upper right with the halo of bright light from the sun on the left bear an obvious resemblance to Picasso's *Minotauromachy* etching of 1935. Louis's drawing can be interpreted as a variation on the form, if not upon the elaborate content, of the Picasso. The famous Spaniard certainly held no exclusive option on the bull-minotaur subject, but Louis's other exploration of that theme in D49A is also notably Picassoid. In this drawing a single eye in the upper center of the page appears to be shared by a densely modeled human head on the left as well as by a bull's head on the right. Thus, instead of indicating a minotaur by placing a bull's head on a human body, Louis apparently attempted to adapt one device Picasso often used to suggest conflicting psychological states by juxtaposing two different heads on either side of a shared profile.

Other drawings from this period reflect Louis's interest in another subject familiar in Picasso's oeuvre: bathers and horses. Drawings D14, D17, and D107 explore this subject, but D107 is particularly Picassoid in that the position of the horse's head and the flattened oval that generates light are both obvious borrowings from *Guernica* and related works, despite the fact that Louis's horse is more dislocated than agonized.[45]

One final drawing that probably owes a debt to Picasso is D65, with its contrasting of densely modeled heads on a fluid, linear figure. This odd figure and the floating, fanciful images around it are similar to a 1927 Picasso etching, used in 1931 as one of the illustrations for Vollard's edition of Balzac's *Le Chef d'oeuvre inconnu*.[46] Like the Picasso etching, the Louis drawing conveys a complex and disturbing psychological content, partially due to the striking contrast between the whimsical, imaginary creatures and the double-headed, reclining man. The wary expression of the crowned figure on the left and the two disembodied female heads certainly exaggerate the tone of a hallucinatory nightmare.

Picasso's work had provided a significant model for many American artists during the 1930s and 1940s, so Louis's interest in it is not surprising. In fact, it must be acknowledged that Louis's turn in this direction about 1948 came at a

Drawing D107 [1948].

Drawing D65 [1948].

time when most of his contemporaries, most notably Pollock, had already moved beyond Picasso's example to break radically new ground. Louis surely had seen Picasso's work during his years in New York, but his paintings and drawings from this period suggest that he was simply not yet ready to absorb lessons from art as advanced as Picasso's. The drawings just examined suggest that after Louis left New York City it was several years before he was able to profit from the older master's work.

Louis's drawings are also evidence that his draftsmanship did not mature until the late 1940s. Picasso was but one of several accomplished draftsmen — Matisse and Miró were two others — who provided valuable models that stimulated Louis's emerging talents. The clumsy masses and stiff, often awkward figures that populated Louis's work in the 1930s and early 1940s began to be replaced about 1948 by both representational and abstract forms rendered with an increasingly assured and fluid line. This is particularly the case with those works in which he allowed his imagination free reign; the subjects drawn from nature continued to be haunted by the inability to "realize" that, according to Charles Schucker, had been a major handicap for Louis during the 1930s.

FLORIDA DRAWINGS, 1948–1949

Despite Louis's reluctance to leave his studio for any purpose, the visits to his family in Florida yielded some of his most successful drawings. His widow recalls that Louis worked in two quite different situations while in Florida. Sometimes they would go to the beach, where he would do contour renderings of bathers he observed; he drew rapidly without lifting his pen from the page. Drawing was, in fact, the only activity he engaged in while at the beach, for he never would go into the water, nor did he even put on a bathing suit or shorts. (Louis was always extremely thin and may simply have been self-conscious, but it is equally likely that he preferred to draw and to remain isolated from the social activities.) In addition to the beach drawings, Louis also worked in the privacy of the guest room of his parents' home, behind a closed door. Based upon the evidence found in two sketchpads purchased in Florida, it appears that this private situation resulted in his most imaginative, dense, and complex drawings, the imagery of which, only partly inspired by the beach scenes, was increasingly transformed into fantastic surrealist visions.

In his drawings from nature, Louis treated the bathers in an exceedingly loose manner, avoiding all specific distinguishing characteristics in favor of a contour line that captured only the most general aspects of the figures' positions. The results are unusually lighthearted and gay, as is evident in the relaxed assurance of the figures in drawing D6, or in the rubbery, impossibly attenuated anatomies of the bathers in D29B, whose proportions and pose recall those of Matisse's 1935 *The Pink Nude*.[47]

Two bathers are also depicted in D69, but the greater specificity in the treatment of the two faces and the nature of the forms with which the bodies are created mark this drawing as an unusual one in Louis's oeuvre.

Drawing D6 [1949].

Drawing D29B [1948].

Henri Matisse, *The Pink Nude*, 1935, oil on canvas, 26 x 36½ inches. The Baltimore Museum of Art, The Cone Collection formed by Dr. Claribel Cone and Miss Etta Cone of Baltimore, Maryland.

(Unfortunately, since it was found as a loose sheet in sketchpad number 12, it is difficult to determine its relationship to the other drawings of bathers.) Louis employed two rapidly drawn curved lines to describe first the shape of the heads and then the facial features, a technique similar to that of the "Budapest String Quartet" drawings. Anatomy is oddly abbreviated, particularly in the figure on the left who appears to lack both hands and torso and consists instead of four or five juxtaposed biomorphic shapes. Even more strange is the conflation of positive and negative space in the torso area, which simultaneously suggests two- and three-dimensionality. His companion is more readily interpreted, despite the curved shape at the juncture of arm and shoulder that suggests both armpit and shoulder blade.

Drawings and paintings by both Matisse and Picasso certainly provided a general influence on Louis's bathers. It is readily apparent, however, that in spite of his obviously developing facility with line, his bathers lack the pervasive sensuality of these European masters, both of whom had consciously extended the odalisque tradition of Ingres and Delacroix. Louis's contour line does not suggest the swelling masses of human anatomy and he chose not to dwell upon the erotic possibilities of his subjects. In fact, quite the contrary, for even the specific sex of his bathers is often open to question. Louis appears to have used the bathers primarily as fluid, two-dimensional shapes; although one can interpret them as relaxed or even indolent, narrative content or psychological interaction is rarely suggested. It is evident that Louis enjoyed himself while making these drawings and, despite the frequent repetition of figures and poses, he generally avoided the staleness of formula in favor of a lively sense of immediacy.

Others of the Florida drawings were probably the product of those periods when he worked in privacy rather than on the beach. As has been observed, when Louis chose to work from his imagination rather than from nature the results were considerably more successful. Some of the Florida drawings suggest that the two groups overlapped, for he appears to have embellished some of his bathers with invented accessories. Drawings D235 and D236, for example, clearly represent bathers, but the hair or hat of one figure (D235) has been transformed into a halo of petals or flames, possibly inspired by a flamboyant beach hat.

Some of these drawings have more to do with a fanciful vision tempered by references to reality than vice versa. In D245, the figure at the left assumes a

Drawing D69 [1948].

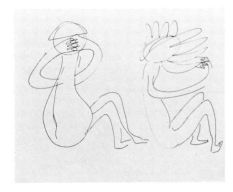

Drawing D235 [1949].

Drawing D245 [1949].

position common to Louis's bathers: viewed from behind, the seated figure raises his arms, clasps his hands behind his head, and crosses his bent legs at the knees. (Perhaps not coincidentally, Louis often assumed this same position.) His companion at the right seems to be female since her body contours are more curvaceous. Seated with her arms crossed in front of her, she rests one leg on the beach, bending it so that her right foot crosses under her raised left leg. At the far right appears a third bather whose smaller scale suggests distance in space. Louis conceived this figure so freely that both its sex and the direction of its pose are ambiguous; the anatomical distortions approximate those of Picasso's bathers of about 1930, but their menacing tone is not present here. The large sun shining brightly in the sky supplements the beach setting, while the high horizon line restricts spatial recession.

But how are we to interpret the remaining forms? Are those in the lower right intended to suggest children playing? Or perhaps beach paraphernalia? Could the shape between the heads of the two bathers be the head of another figure that was begun and then abandoned by the artist? And what are we to make of the strange triad of abstract biomorphic shapes near the horizon? Since these forms all remain ambiguous they prompt questions as to the degree of Louis's commitment to the quotidian beach scene as his primary subject.

One can only hypothesize now, thirty years after the fact, about the manner in which Louis's ideas developed. It seems likely, however, that he proceeded from the mundane to the fantastic. Beginning with bathers drawn from nature, he apparently began to improvise, first by treating the figures themselves with increasing freedom and later by adding other elements, the natural sources of which (if there were any) are now obscured in forms that have assumed a new life as abstract shapes. Some of those abstract configurations, such as the biomorphic triad in D245, reappear in other drawings in much the same manner as the more figurative images.

An entire subgroup of Florida fantasies are populated by a whimsical horned "antelope" which may owe its original conception to a hornlike ponytail sported by one of the bathers in drawing D23. This droll antelope also appears in drawings D4, D11, D39, and D237, almost without modification, always gazing searchingly into the sky. In D237, despite the biomorphic triad familiar from the beach fantasies, the subject seems to have been shifted in the direction of a nocturnal hunt in which a figure armed with a bow and

Drawing D23 [1949].

Drawing D11 [1949].

Drawing D237 [1949].

arrow pursues his prey under the moon. Perhaps Louis intended this as a gentle nod in the direction of the mythic subjects explored by Pollock and other abstract expressionists in the early 1940s.

If we had not previously observed the development of this bizarre cast of characters, drawing D39 might not make much iconographical sense. Since this is the only drawing in the group that Louis signed and dated (1949), he presumably considered it important.[48] Certainly one would not have to decipher the entire subject in order to appreciate the technique of the drawing and the enchanting nature of its invented forms. We are, however, particularly fortunate to possess not only the group of drawings generally related to this one, but also D248, which is its "preparatory study" and shares its same disposition of major shapes without their elaborate modeling.

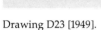

Drawing D39, 1949. Mrs. Moses Siegel, Washington, D.C.

Drawing D248 [1949].

Once accustomed to Louis's formal vocabulary it is easy to identify as standing bathers the figures at far right and left in D248, but their transformation in D39 nearly obliterates their original identity. The left-hand figure now hovers in midair, seemingly only a cluster of abstract ovals and spirals. In contrast, the right-hand figure has assumed a far greater degree of three dimensionality due to the modeling that describes its different facets; this figure's clasped hands, still evident in D248, are totally absent in D39, in which it now resembles a carved wooden assemblage with a flowerlike head. Once again Picasso's work is brought to mind, particularly his series of drawings from 1933 titled "An Anatomy," which similarly depict humanoid assemblages created from both pliant and sculptural forms. Picasso also used the inverted moon shape to suggest a torso similar to that of Louis's flower-headed figure.

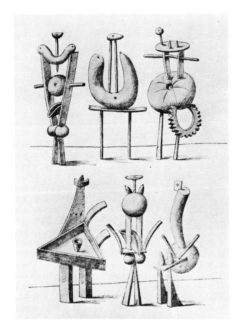

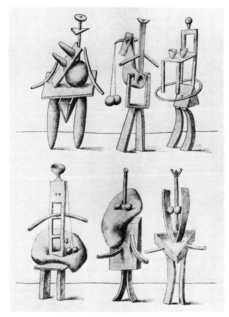

Pablo Picasso, *An Anatomy*, 1932, pencil on paper, dimensions unknown. Reproduced in *Minotaure*, no. 1 (1933).

Pablo Picasso, *An Anatomy*, 1932, pencil on paper, dimensions unknown. Reproduced in *Minotaure*, no. 1 (1933).

The other two vertical figures in D248 are not readily identified as bathers and their elaboration in D39 suggests that Louis never thought of them as such. The center shape was transformed from one drawing to the other into a stargazing antelope with a curly mane. The belly of the horned animal was rendered not as a simple volume but as an agitated swirl of curved and looping lines. Even more fanciful is its companion, a disembodied, dancing lobster claw, the shape and position of which echo those of the antelope's raised head. In the earlier drawing only the two-dimensional contour of this shape was suggested and it was only in a second stage that Louis imparted imaginative life to it. Similarly the biomorphic triad appears in both versions but demonstrates greater specificity of contour and modeling in D39. When these major figures are supplemented by the other images in the drawing, especially the menacing oyster shell on the beach, the metamorphosis into surrealist fantasy is complete. It is perfectly evident, however, that the violence so often characteristic of that style was rejected by Louis in favor of a more humorous and genial vision. In spite of their greater degree of abstraction, drawings D44, D233A, and #507 convey a similar mood.

Although the whimsical quality of D39 suggests a fantastic daydream, others of the similarly elaborate drawings from the same period reflect a vision more akin to a nightmare. Drawing D46 for example, and its preparatory study, D45, share with the previous work the biomorphic triad, but the arch has become noticeably more attenuated. The primary shape it encloses resembles a shrimp in D46 but possesses a menacing saw-tooth belly in D45. The images that emerge from the dense hatching of D46 lack the droll quality of the antelope and dancing lobster claw; instead, a horizontal creature with pointed ears and bulging eyes hovers threateningly in the sky, an apparition

Drawing D233A [1949].

44

witnessed by a slightly more human figure who moves off to the right in escape.

Drawing D41, certainly a nightmarish vision, depicts a human figure stretched horizontally across the entire top of the page, its hands seemingly bound, its gaze fixed upon something off in the distance, and its body floating free of the gravitational force that holds the other figures in a vertical position. Of the six figures below, the most obvious is a woman in the center whose vertically positioned eyes repeat a distortion often employed by Picasso. Drawing D40A also presents a frightening scene in which a huge, disembodied eye with a lid of flames is pursued by a host of menacing figures, all of whom chase a tall, thin figure off to the left.

The more abstract of these Florida drawings, such as D43, are also more neutral in mood, lacking either the fanciful or the alarming aspects just described. In this example, despite the proliferation of abstract shapes, it is evident that Louis had not totally abandoned the beach scene, for the horizon line is still present and a sun (or moon) appears in the sky. Indeed, a Henry Moore-like figure can be perceived sprawling across the lower right corner. Two other figures emerge from the dense network, standing in the distance on the horizon; the torso of one is described by a single line that connects a flattened, semicircular head to the oval of the arms and the dark triangle that forms its base.

Other related drawings significantly undermine the partitioning of the space by a horizon line, as is evident in D40A where it appears quite close to the bottom edge, and also in D43 where it can barely be distinguished. Drawings D42, D44, and #507 dispense entirely with a land/sky division; instead, the page is treated as a continuous field on which Louis floated increasingly abstract images. It is evident that his imagery was here derived far more from the process of automatic drawing than from a distant subject in nature. He appears to have eased himself gradually into this liberating technique, using it first to embellish the background or selected figures before exploiting it to the utmost.

Louis's 1948–49 surrealist fantasies, clearly the most complex and inventive of his drawings, also represent his highest achievement in the drawing

Drawing D46 [1949].

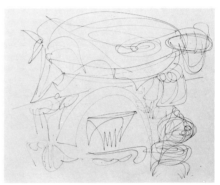

Drawing D45 [1949].

Drawing D41 [1949].

Drawing D43 [1949].

45

medium. Some of his later drawings did provide him with important lessons as he moved increasingly toward an entirely abstract vocabulary and some of them are significant works in themselves. But none of these later drawings possesses the combination of freshness, spontaneity, and imaginative wealth as some of those from 1948–49.

Certainly, part of their success arises from the tension between nature and the imaginary, between the figurative and the abstract that Louis exploited so thoroughly. It was precisely this tension that had increasingly permeated so much painting in New York earlier in the 1940s when many artists explored the possibilities that emerged from the synthesis of cubism and surrealism. Gorky was the first of them to create a major oeuvre from this synthesis; his death in 1948 was a particular loss for his contemporaries. At that very moment Pollock embarked upon his first major series of paintings in which figurative imagery was entirely abandoned in favor of a suggestive, calligraphic network that alone carried both form and content. Barnett Newman, Clyfford Still, and Mark Rothko similarly found increasingly viable abstract vocabularies, which so thoroughly altered the very nature of American painting that, by comparison, Gorky has come to be perceived as an "old master."

In his surrealist drawings Louis is closer to Gorky and, through him, to Miró, than he is to Pollock. This reflects both Louis's retention of a relatively naturalistic space and imagery as well as the manner in which the forms were discovered. It remains difficult to determine whether Louis was directly

Untitled, circa 1948, acrylic on canvas,
25 x 30⅛ inches. Private collection.

Joan Miró, *Woman and Kite among the Constellations*, 1939, oil on burlap, 31⅞ x 23⅝ inches. Collection of Mrs. Hildegard Ault Tjeder.

influenced by either Miró or Gorky or if his work simply followed a similar pattern of development at a later date, but the relationship is such that direct influence seems likely.

During his years in New York, Louis must have seen exhibitions of Miró's work, including the 1941 major retrospective at the Museum of Modern Art, because Miró was one of the European artists most admired by painters in New York. As has already been suggested with regard to Louis's experiencing of Picasso's work, he was not prepared to absorb influence from avant-garde European art when he first encountered it. That he later became seriously interested in Miró is demonstrated not only in the drawings, but even more directly in an untitled painting of about 1948, where both the imagery and the manner in which the paint was squeezed directly from the tube onto the canvas are decidedly Miroesque. In fact, Miró's *Women and Kite among the Constellations* (1939), which was included in the 1941 retrospective, is a possible precedent for the Louis painting.

Although Louis may have learned from Miró's example, it is unlikely that he knew how close to the Spaniard he was in the manner in which he derived the imagery of his fantasy drawings. For example, another Miró painting included in the retrospective, entitled *Portrait of Mistress Mills in 1750* (1929), based upon an engraving after a painting by George Engleheart,[49] evolved from a series of drawings beginning with a relatively naturalistic rendering that was gradually transformed into a whimsical creature owing as much to Miró's imagination as to the original source. Louis could not have known about this process of transformation, since it was only in 1973 that Miró gave the drawings to the Museum of Modern Art, but Louis's transformation of bathers into images of fantasy followed a related pattern. Picasso, of course, also used this technique as one of the major ways in which he generated imagery.

Louis's formal vocabulary and pictorial complexities in the 1948–49 drawings are even closer to Arshile Gorky's work. Louis's widow reports that he greatly admired Gorky, and Louis himself claimed that he knew Gorky in New York during the 1930s, according to the résumé that he prepared in 1952. Louis could not, however, have seen many of Gorky's mature paintings or drawings by 1949, when his own drawings were closest in appearance to them. If the two men really were acquainted, Louis may have visited Gorky's studio in New York in the 1930s and he could have seen examples of the work in the Whitney annuals during the late 1930s and early 1940s. Since Louis left New York in 1944 or 1945, it is unlikely that he saw the exhibitions of Gorky's work held annually at the Julien Levy Gallery between 1945 and 1948. Nevertheless, the related imagery and technique of certain examples of the two men's work appear too close to be accidental.

As Ethel Schwabacher and others have suggested, and Harry Rand has demonstrated,[50] Gorky's apparently obscure or abstract imagery sometimes came from entirely quotidian sources or from forms in nature viewed at extremely close range. Often proceeding in a serial fashion, Gorky would repeat the same imagery in drawings where the original source is relatively obvious and in paintings in which the images were increasingly veiled or subjected to simplification, editing, or transformation. Works on common themes that demonstrate this type of development include the series "The Calendars," "The Garden in Sochi," and "The Plow and the Song." Louis was

Joan Miró, Cartoon for *Portrait of Mistress Mills in 1750*, 1929, charcoal and pencil on paper, 24 5/8 x 19 inches. The Museum of Modern Art, New York; gift of the artist.

certainly not as programmatical in his procedure as Gorky, but his repetition of certain images in drawings that otherwise reflect an increasing "fantastification" echoes Gorky's method.

Certain of Louis's drawings from 1949 bear a remarkable similarity to some of Gorky's drawings from the "Nighttime Enigma and Nostalgia" series from the early 1930s.[51] The relationship between the two drawings from this series illustrated here is extremely similar to that between Louis's drawings D39 and D248 (see pp. 42–43): a rapidly executed contour rendering provided the basic forms upon which the artist lavished his attention in the other densely modeled work. Furthermore, if one compares Louis's drawing D43 (see p. 45) with Gorky's *Objects,* one discovers an analogous vocabulary of biomorphic shapes that emerge from and are embedded into the elaborate, dense crosshatching of the background field. Shapes seemingly inspired by the sculpture of Arp are also common to both. The velvety richness of the dark areas, used so effectively by both artists as a foil for the crisp clarity of contour lines, evokes effects achieved in engravings or etchings.[52]

Louis's surrealist fantasy drawings occupy a crucial place in his artistic development. For the first time he relaxed his dependence on nature in order to give his imagination free reign. In so doing he turned to the surrealist technique of automatic drawing, which generated a wealth of suggestive biomorphic forms. No longer strictly bound to naturalistic space, he began to float images on a densely hatched, shallow field with spatial ambiguities similar to those later explored in his Veil paintings. The obvious relationship between some of the bather images drawn from nature and the fantasy images makes it evident that he was consciously exploring the synthesis that proved so central to the development of American painting: first, a surrealist exploitation and elaboration of formal analogies and, second, a cubist simplification and abstraction of forms observed in nature. Louis's willingness to confront this issue signals a commitment to the artistic vanguard not previously evident in his work; his paintings and drawings of the four or five subsequent years reflect his gradual resolution of this issue and the search for a personal solution.

Arshile Gorky, *Study for Nighttime Enigma and Nostalgia,* circa 1931–32, pencil on paper, 22¼ x 28¾ inches. The Museum of Modern Art, New York; gift of Richard S. Zeisler.

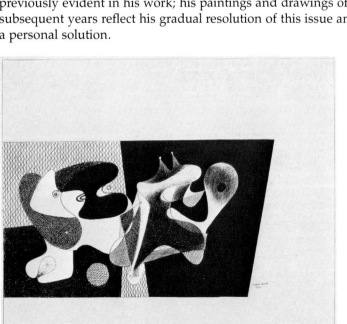

Arshile Gorky, *Objects,* 1932, pen and ink on paper, 22¼ x 30 inches. The Museum of Modern Art, New York; Van Gogh Purchase Fund.

FIGURATIVE AND ABSTRACT DRAWINGS, 1950–1953

About 1950 Louis produced a group of drawings containing figures that are distant cousins of the "Budapest String Quartet" drawings of a few years earlier. Unlike these previous examples, the later figures are not caricatures based upon living models but are instead imaginary conceptions from the outset. Stick-thin torsos supported by loosely rendered feet that resemble the base of a tripod are evident in the pairs of figures in drawings D189A, D191A, D196A, D475, and D476. In each instance these triangular-headed creatures stand under a moon (or sun) and stars. In D475, the head of the figure on the right dangles like a pendant from the pointed tip of the adjoining shape and he appears to adopt a pose deferential to his companion. Louis's formal

Drawing D475 [1950].

language again bears striking affinities with that of Miró, who used a similar vocabulary in paintings like *The Hunter (Catalan Landscape)* (1923–24), and that of Gorky, whose paintings and drawings from such series as "The Calendars" (1946–47) and "The Betrothal" (1947) are populated with kindred spirits.

Miró may also have been one inspiration that encouraged Louis to float abstract forms, stars, suns, moons, and disconnected decorative lines across the page, their even dispersal canceling any spatial recession. Even more effective in this regard is Louis's use of regularly spaced horizontal lines like those in D475; in this drawing they were drawn freehand, perhaps beginning with a single line that would have suggested a horizon. By 1953, however, he often relied on a ruler to produce a measured pattern, often a grid, which functioned as a counterpoint to the loosely rendered images beneath it, a composing device that will be examined below.

While D475 contains clearly recognizable figures on the abstract, flattened field, D180 reveals considerably more abstract creatures set into a space conceived more like a landscape. The two large figures and one small one at the far right are composed of cascading links, both ovoid and triangular, that replace the linear torso of the previous group. These more freely rendered forms are set in a containing "window" or frame through which one views the curving scribbles of the foreground, the horizontals of the middle ground, and the dotted area of "sky." The frame, however, breaks at the bottom, permitting the foreground to spill out, effectively denying the spatial illusion.

That Louis intended the looped, cascading lines of D180 to suggest figures is made obvious by comparing it to D232, in which two notably Miroesque creatures at the right are joined by two densely rendered, abstract images at

Joan Miró, *The Hunter (Catalan Landscape)*, 1923–24, oil on canvas, 25½ x 39½ inches. The Museum of Modern Art, New York; purchase.

Drawing D180 [1950].

Drawing D232 [1953].

50

the left, their identity as humans suggested by a similar spatial placement in relation to the ground line, starry border, and background screen or curtain. The curvilinear assemblage at the far right would seem to be the female companion of the triangular-headed, angular male beside her.

This "female" bears a remarkable — though likely coincidental — similarity to the image in David Smith's preliminary sketches for *Tanktotem III* (from a notebook of about 1950–54). Louis's figure, like all of Smith's, is a totem intended to be perceived as a female.[53] The relationship, whether accidental or not, raises the question of how we are to interpret Louis's figures in this drawing and the ones previously discussed. No evidence suggests that Louis, like Smith, Pollock, and other abstract expressionists, was interested in pictorial imagery that directly reflected the psychoanalytic theory or symbolism explored in the writings of Freud and Jung. Certainly, the general formal simplification of Louis's figures and their ever-increasing abstraction is consistent with ideas explored by many abstract expressionists during the 1940s, but it would be inappropriate to impose on Louis's work an interpretation borrowed from the work and philosophies of other artists. Louis knew about psychoanalytic theory in general terms, as did most educated people, and one of his friends was a psychologist. But the fantasy creatures that populate his drawings from the late 1940s and early 1950s do not appear to reflect hidden psychological content. Indeed, it is likely that the relaxed, often humorous tone of Louis's figures, which is quite opposed to the strain or intensity so characteristic of Pollock's work, is a result of Louis's greater interest in the form rather than the deeply buried content of his images. Both the imagery and technique of most of Louis's drawings reflect a sense of ease and well-being that suggest he viewed drawing as a time filler and not as a means for probing his innermost being.

A number of extant paintings contemporaneous with the drawings under discussion demonstrate that Louis was exploring closely related ideas in the two mediums. His interest in translating the concepts of drawing directly into painting had appeared at least as early as about 1948, when he executed the Miroesque painting described above in which the paint was actually squeezed from the tube onto the canvas. *The Ladder* (1950) is also indebted to Miró's work, although in more abstract terms; it may be the earliest of Louis's works to include a grid, which was apparently created here by dripping black paint over the more densely painted blue background. This technique yielded a slack network that is far more relaxed in configuration than the carefully ruled grids of the later drawings.

Even closer in style and imagery to the drawings are the series of "Charred Journal" paintings from 1951, five of which were included in Louis's exhibition in 1953 at the Washington Workshop.[54] The pictures in this series share with the drawings of the period the placement of loosely conceived, incipiently figurative linear images set against a gridded background plane. In the paintings the grid was produced both by dripping black paint and by a far more unusual method. According to Leon Berkowitz, Louis reported that the subtle grid pattern evident in these pictures was achieved by pressing lengths of toilet paper into the wet paint of the background.[55]

Louis also told Berkowitz and the critics who reviewed the 1953 exhibition that the titles for the "Charred Journal" series referred to the Nazi book burnings.[56] The imagery of the pictures is more suggestive than descriptive,

David Smith, *Sketches for Tanktotem III*, circa 1950–54, pen and ink and ink wash on paper, 10¾ x 16½ inches. David Smith Papers, Archives of American Art, Smithsonian Institution, Washington, D.C.

Charred Journal —Firewritten I, 1951, acrylic on canvas, 39 x 30⅜ inches. Daniel Millsaps, Washington, D.C.

Charred Journal —Firewritten Untitled A, 1951, acrylic on canvas, 36⅛ x 30 inches.

Charred Journal —Firewritten Untitled B, 1951, acrylic on canvas, 36⅛ x 30 inches.

with the evocation of Roman numerals and a variety of abstract symbols and biomorphic figures rendered in white paint on the generally black ground. Louis told his wife that he had tried to capture the effect of letters and symbols rising like ashes from the surface of a burned page. Although these paintings have sometimes been cited as evidence of Louis's response to Pollock's work, it appears that Miró's adaptation of surrealist automatism is closer to their spirit; the easel scale of the pictures, their lyrical rather than aggressive tone (despite the subject), and the openness rather than density of the space are all more akin to Miró than to Pollock.

Precisely when Louis first saw Pollock's work in the original is not certain. Clement Greenberg believes that Louis knew the work only by means of reproductions until his trip to New York in April 1953. In addition to exhibition reviews that contained photographs of the work, Louis may have seen the May 1951 issue of *Art News* that contained Robert Goodnough's article "Pollock Paints a Picture," illustrated by Hans Namuth's photographs of the artist at work on *Autumn Rhythm.* But the paintings by Pollock that are closest to Louis's "Charred Journal" series are the black-and-white pictures, which were first exhibited as a group at the Betty Parsons Gallery late in 1951 and thus probably not known to Louis when his own series was painted. A hotel receipt found among Louis's papers, however, indicates that he was in New York on April 12–13, 1951. It is impossible to know what museums or galleries he may have visited, but it is possible that he saw the Whitney annual, which ran from March 17 to May 6; if so, he could have seen Pollock's watercolor *Number 1, 1951.* Also on view during those two days was an exhibition called "Sculpture by Painters" at the Peridot Gallery, which included both a painting and a papier-mâché sculpture by Pollock.[57]

During precisely the period when Pollock was turning away from radical abstraction to reinvestigate the evocative, totemic imagery of his earlier work, Louis began to pursue the abstract potential of his imagery. The Miroesque

Drawing D302, 1953.

Drawing D399, 1953.

figures of such drawings as D475 (see p. 49) and D232 (see p. 50) reappear as wholly abstract, cascading loops in several 1953 drawings, including D291, D302, and D399. Suggestions of naturalistic space are entirely absent, replaced in D291, for example, by two grid layers (a freehand one in ink and a ruled one in pencil) and a pattern of crossing diagonals. Symbolic clues such as eyes, moon/sun, or stars have been eliminated although several related drawings (D290, D293, D295, D302, D404) employ the arabic numerals 1, 2, and 3. Of course, by 1953 numbers were not unusual elements in drawings or paintings since they had been used by the cubists and futurists, and by Pollock, de Kooning, and other artists who exploited them for both iconographical and formal purposes. Louis's specific intention is unknown, but he appears to have equated numbers with stars and small x's as simply another form of symbolic notation. In addition, he often used them as a foil for the letters and numbers of his signature and date.

Of all the drawings examined thus far, D399 is the most abstract in appearance. Natural space and imagery are entirely abandoned in favor of an equalization of figuration across the page. The pattern of thick, staccato marks that resemble Hebrew script contributes to the dematerialization of the drawing. Louis's positive response to this and many others of the 1953 drawings is indicated by his decision to sign and date a number of them; in fact, of his fifty-eight signed and dated works on paper, fifty-one are inscribed with the year 1953.

For Louis as a draftsman, 1953 was an unusually productive year, one in which about 150 of his extant drawings were executed. As has been suggested, one likely reason for this was that money for painting supplies was in short supply. Another likely reason is his decision to exhibit drawings in his one-man show that year, which may have prompted him to devote particular energy to drawing. It is uncertain precisely which drawings were exhibited, but one very likely possibility is *Geometry of a Fish* (D215), the only drawing on

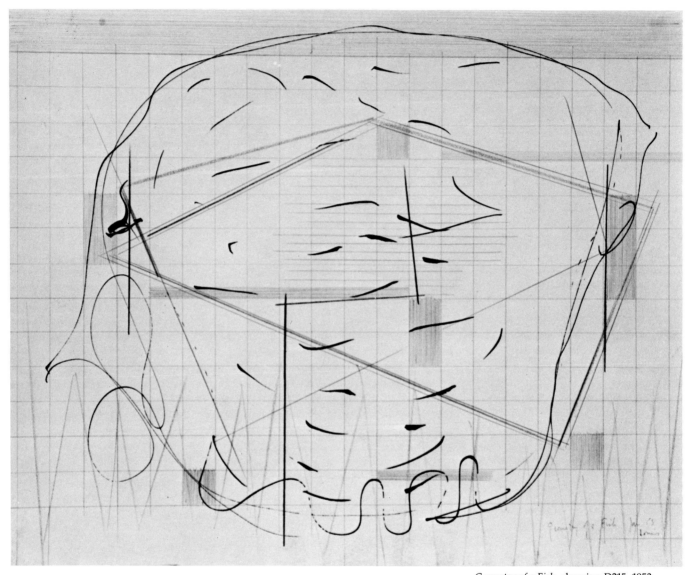

Geometry of a Fish, drawing D215, 1953.

which Louis inscribed a title. He also signed the work and dated it January 1953, the most specific date found on any of his works on paper. Both the title and the image emphasize with great clarity the duality explored consistently in the drawings of that year: the contrast between a freely conceived, centered image and a superimposed, usually carefully ruled grid.

Since this grid, already observed as a feature in several earlier works, becomes a consistent element in 1953, it merits consideration in its own right. Precisely what prompted him to use this device so frequently remains unknown, but several hypotheses have emerged. His widow, who once taught geography, believes that it reflects Louis's interest in maps and, therefore, suggests that the grid lines could be interpreted as lines of latitude and longitude. I have been unable, however, to identify other elements in the drawings that support the map analogy.

The grid might reflect Louis's adaptation of the traditional device employed to facilitate the transfer of images from preparatory studies to a canvas or wall support. Old master drawings were frequently gridded for this purpose and Gorky often worked in a similar manner. But the evidence suggests that Louis did not, for none of his extant drawings can be considered a preparatory study for any extant painting. In fact, the "Charred Journal" paintings indicate that Louis viewed grids as integral parts of his pictorial conception and not as ancillary features.

Another possible source for the grid was suggested to me by Michael Fried, who was reminded of D'Arcy Thompson's *On Growth and Form* when he first saw Louis's drawings a number of years ago.[58] Although it is known that Pollock admired this book, which he received as a gift from Tony Smith,[59] whether or not Louis was familiar with it remains unknown. Thompson's final chapter, "On the Theory of Transformations, or the Comparison of Related Forms," does contain illustrations of fish whose morphological relation is expressed by altering coordinates of a grid on which they are drawn and, thereby, altering the fish shapes accordingly. The resulting images and the presence of grids that are both taut and elastic are perhaps coincidentally related to Louis's drawings.

More likely as an influence are some photocollages Louis made in 1950 for a commission he received from the United States Public Health Service. His design for a tuberculosis display panel for a medical convention employs a compelling image: the shadow of a standing man (only the feet of whom can be seen in the upper right corner) stretches diagonally downward and left across a sidewalk, with the vertical and horizontal divisions between its cement sections providing a stark foil for the human silhouette. Louis heightened the dramatic impact by surrealistically superimposing a chest X-ray on the shadow's chest area. In order to emphasize the contrast between rectilinear and curvilinear elements, Louis gave the photocollage a biomorphic shape, the orientation of which, like that of the shadow, runs counter to the sidewalk pattern. Formal compositional devices successfully invoke drama and tension appropriate for the subject.[60]

Louis's use of the grid was by no means unique, for it had emerged during the 1940s in the work of several abstract expressionists, Adolph Gottlieb and William Baziotes among them, who were attempting to break free of the cubist elements that had dominated their early work. But in their work the grid formed an integral part of the composition as it imposed order on the forms it circumscribed. Louis, on the other hand, conceived his central image first and only later superimposed the grid. He established a confrontation more than a synthesis of two opposed systems: the one, rectilinear and rational; the other, curvilinear and imaginative.

Adopting the fish as subject matter is less surprising than the consistent appearance of the grid. Louis had used this fish as early as 1948 in *Sub-Marine*, an oil painting that was awarded a prize when he exhibited it in 1949 at the Baltimore Museum. The subject may have appealed to Louis simply because it was a fluid, easily rendered shape. The visits to Florida, which began at that time, may also have provided an immediate stimulus. Louis's widow recalls that on one such visit he reluctantly agreed to a ride on a glass-bottomed boat; its viewing platform would have presented a regular structure through which fish were viewed, a situation analogous to the grid and fish in the drawing of 1953.

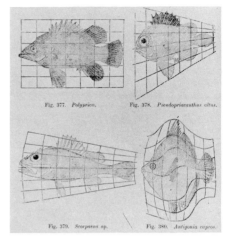

D'Arcy Wentworth Thompson, *On Growth and Form* [Cambridge: Cambridge University Press, 1917], illustration, page 750.

Untitled, 1950, photocollage, 12 x 9 inches.

Unlike the carefully conceived *Geometry of a Fish,* other fish drawings are spontaneous in execution, as is evident in D360, in which rapidly sketched lines suggest a striped fish and the bubbles it generated in the water. The fish shape of D348 is similar, but the artist added a freehand grid and other marks including stars and the symbols for addition, subtraction, and number. Drawing D346 expands the symbolic vocabulary with a six-pointed Star of David and a carefully ruled grid superimposed on the other images. The abstract, intellectual content implied by these symbols is defied by the splattering of orange ink or watercolor, which suggests both the markings of a tropical fish and an irrational, spontaneous gesture.

The fish images of these drawings are closely related both to *Sub-Marine* and to a second extremely similar painting, presumably destroyed by Louis but preserved in a photograph in which the inscription "Louis 48" is evident in the lower right corner. In both pictures a large fish and smaller aquatic creatures were drawn on a field of rectilinear and curvilinear planes that fit together like large pieces of a jigsaw puzzle. In *Sub-Marine* these planes are predominantly gray, but vivid areas of yellow-orange roughly coincide with the fish. These paintings, more than the drawings, bear certain affinities with treatments of related themes by Baziotes and Rothko, notably in the delicacy of line and the coloristic subtleties of the field. In addition, the paintings project an interest in the primordial suggestiveness of the sea imagery that was also shared by the abstract expressionists. And also like them, Louis attempted to effect a synthesis between the discipline of cubism and the freedom of surrealist-inspired drawing. Louis's later drawings of fish are not

Sub-Marine, 1948, oil on canvas, 23 x 36 inches. Private collection, Hillsborough, North Carolina.

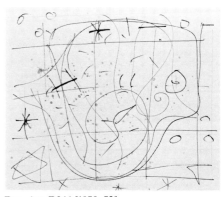

Drawing D346 [1950–53].

Drawing D360 [1950–53].

similarly laden with implied content and appear more light-hearted, with an interest in form seemingly dominating that in meaning.

Other drawings of 1953, such as D347 and D415, transform the large, central shape into one that is less fishlike. Symbolic markings are more specific, however, and it becomes difficult not to interpret them as forming short words ("Hi") or Roman numerals (X, XI). The compositions and signs suggest analogies with Gottlieb's pictographs, although Louis's forms are more abstract. The effect, nonetheless, is similar, for one senses that the configuration possesses a "meaning" even though no specific decoding is possible. Louis was apparently as interested as other artists of his generation in exploiting forms of writing and symbolic notation as a viable model for pursuing a greater degree of abstraction without abandoning the more obvious content of figurative art. It is intriguing to recall that his experience with the PWAP mural of 1934 had introduced Louis to many primitive forms of writing, a circumstance that preceded by several years the widespread interest in this subject on the part of New York artists.[61] And, of course, his "Charred Journal" paintings had employed a closely related vocabulary of signs and symbols in a context that made explicit the analogy to written language.

Geometry of a Fish was obviously conceived more carefully than the other fish drawings from its beginning, since its features are all rendered less spontaneously. Louis worked deliberately, creating the fish from two roughly parallel lines that resulted in a shape that is ponderous in contrast to the buoyancy of the previous fish images. Fluctuating lines suggest a ventral fin, and short, thick lines across the body provide its markings. Scattered symbolic notations are absent, having been replaced by the specific inscription, precise grid, and other rectilinear configurations. Small sections of the grid, such as the top margin of the page, are shaped by meticulously ruled lines drawn extremely close together. The shaded grid sections are connected by two irregular polygons drawn in green pencil to produce a total shape that roughly corresponds to the fish. It becomes obvious that Louis has described the fish in two different visual languages, superimposing the one on the other; the silhouette as it might be perceived in nature provides the two-dimensional shape, while the geometrical framework of polygons that appear to recede in space suggests the three-dimensional mass. The two systems are so integrated by the transparency of the rendering that they cannot be perceived independently. Geometric and organic forms enrich each other to create a whole that is more allusive than either. In a considerably more subtle and successful manner, Louis's Veil paintings of 1958 benefit from a similar wedding (by means of transparency) of measured structure and organic form.

Louis's exploration of a large, centered shape in his drawings of 1953 yielded a number of elephant images in addition to the fish. Many of the same compositional and formal devices discussed above are also evident in such drawings as D270 and D275, but the indentation along the bottom of the central shape eliminates any resemblance to a fish. This new form evolved from drawings like D478, which can be readily interpreted as an elephant with an eye and trunk on the left, tiny tail on the right, massive legs, and textured hide.

It is obvious that Louis was no more concerned with the detailed description of an elephant than was Baziotes when the latter tried to "depict"

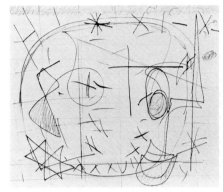

Drawing D347 [1950–53].

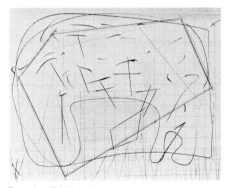

Drawing D275 [1953].

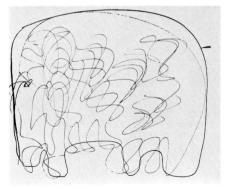

Drawing D478 [1950].

William Baziotes, *Cyclops*, 1947, oil on canvas, 48 x 40 inches. The Art Institute of Chicago, Illinois.

Cyclops, 1950, oil on canvas, dimensions unknown. Private collection.

a rhinoceros in his painting *Cyclops* (1947), although Ethel Baziotes recalls that a pachyderm in the Bronx Zoo was an inspiration for her husband's picture.[62] For Baziotes the beast carried overtones of primordial creatures and the famous race of one-eyed Cyclopes of Greek mythology. At one time Louis shared this interest, for in 1950 he executed a painting entitled *Cyclops*, which has a massive, dark figure in the center that is easily interpreted as a giant, one-eyed beast. Mythological overtones are not, however, present in the elephant drawings, in which the ponderous form lacks the forcefulness of the 1950 painting. Indeed, the speed of rendering and predominantly light touch impart an element of humor to it.

The formal principles of the fish and elephant drawings propelled Louis into nonfiguration in much the same way as had his totemic Miroesque figures. The large central images in D218 and D366, for example, no longer suggest either aquatic or zoomorphic creatures. Freed from all vestiges of figural pretext these drawings witness the expansion of Louis's vocabulary by introducing a diverse range of markings and symbols that are increasingly

Drawing D366 [1950–53].

Drawing D260, 1953.

58

dispersed more evenly across the page. The sometimes uncomfortable tension in the fish and elephant drawings between the specificity of subject and its nonobjective, geometric framework is now avoided by a thorough exploitation of a purely pictorial tension between curvilinear, freely rendered elements and a rectilinear, controlled superstructure. Drawing D366 projects such a striking degree of kinesthetic activity that it may be interpreted as an energy or electrical force field.

Drawing D317 [1950–53].

Equally energetic, although in a more compelling manner, is drawing D260, where a central mass barely contains the vigor of the rendering. Louis must have been agitated or even anguished when he made this drawing, for he bore down terribly hard on the pencil and used the yellow pencil more freely than in any other drawing. Previously both yellow and green pencil were employed solely to fill in a carefully circumscribed shape or to accent a ruled line. But here the color was applied with the same vitality as the graphite. Even the signature is nearly spasmodic, adding to the sensation of incipient explosion. In a related vein, sketchpad number 11 is filled with drawings, including D317, in which the striking vitality of free-form images is countered by the measured repetition of ruled lines. First spontaneously and then compulsively, Louis traced and retraced the major shapes in ink and colored pencil. These images are so totally nonfigurative, and Louis exercised such freedom with regard to the placement of the shaded margin, stars, and ruled lines, that the proper orientation of the pages remains ambiguous. The fact that he did not commit himself to any single orientation by signing any of the drawings in this group may indicate that he preferred to leave that issue undecided; if so, this introduces an uncharacteristic aspect of freedom not previously evident in his oeuvre.

Louis's lack of money for paint and canvas in 1953 led him to brief experiments in collage and acrylic paintings on paper in addition to the profusion of drawings. He was so satisfied with three of his four (known) collages that he included them in the Washington Workshop exhibition where they were titled *Tranquilities I, II,* and *III*.[63] Using an upsom board support, which was as large as thirty-six by seventy-two inches in one instance, he attached dress pattern tissue paper painted with acrylic paint in a limited palette of neutral gray, black, and brown. The inherent translucency of the tissue was fully exploited in compositions in which a few circular forms are dominated by a vertical and horizontal structure that recalls the work of Robert Motherwell. Less derivative, but ultimately less successful, are three paintings on paper (D499, D500, and #508), the palette of which is also restricted to neutrals. In two of the three, Louis used a wide brush and floated crude, calligraphic forms on the page, permitting broad areas of unpainted paper to provide buoyancy for the forms. In the third, D500, he covered the page more completely, carefully framing the larger, central forms with a painted border; the layered application of paint yielded a range of values within the single color and makes this the strongest of the three. Louis was evidently pleased with each, however, for they are all signed and dated.[64]

Although the compositional principles of the collages and paintings on paper relate to general ideas introduced in the drawings, Louis transformed those concepts to explore the unique potentials of the three different mediums. This reflects a change in attitude from the "Charred Journal" paintings of a few years earlier, which were painted linear renderings of the

Drawing D500, 1953.

formal and figural conceptions of his contemporary drawings. No broad generalizations can be offered about the relationship between Louis's drawings of 1953 and his paintings of that year. Only four of the latter are extant, and none pursues the linearity of the previous paintings nor of the contemporary drawings. Although he did not eliminate draftsmanship as a concern after 1953, Louis apparently ceased to execute drawings. Further, for a number of years his paintings reflected a subjugation of drawing per se to a concern with color. Not until 1960 did he return to explore in paintings the potential for drawing in his innovative and powerful Unfurled series, an example of which, *Delta Kappa,* is illustrated. Those pictures were neither preceded nor accompanied by small-scale studies on paper, but emerged instead from other paintings that served as studies in which the issues of composition, color, and draftsmanship were tackled full scale (see *Phi*).[65]

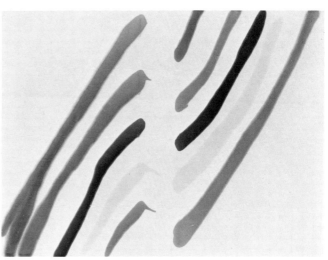

Delta Kappa, 1960, acrylic on canvas, 103¼ x
146 inches.

Phi, 1960–61, acrylic on canvas, 104¼ x 142½
inches.

CONCLUSION

An essay on Morris Louis written in 1965 that placed him "at the juncture of
two traditions" was more accurate than its author could have known, for his
assessment is materially substantiated by the drawings, which were then
largely unknown.[66] The essay explored the dilemma that the Guggenheim
memorial exhibition in 1963 posed for those of Louis's earliest admirers who
had just accepted and praised him as an "optical, color-as-form" painter on
the basis of his Stripe paintings of 1961–62. His Veil paintings of 1958 that were
shown at the Guggenheim, however, appeared to reflect a sensibility far more
akin to the "color-field" paintings of the New York school. Thus, Louis
appeared to be an artist of both the 1950s and 1960s, but the acceptance of one
group of his paintings as valid seemed to some viewers at the time to question
the seriousness of the other group. Evidence of continuity in his paintings was
not readily apparent.

   Louis's early development, as revealed for the first time in these drawings,
echoed a general pattern of distillation characteristic of the careers of most
abstract expressionists. When viewed in the context of his life during the same
period this conclusion comes as no surprise, for he shared many experiences
common to artists of the New York school. He, too, struggled through the
Great Depression, found financial and artistic sustenance in the WPA,
participated in Artists' Union activities. He, too, eventually turned to major
European twentieth-century masters such as Picasso, Miró, and Matisse to
find his way beyond a provincial heritage. His work reflects a gradual shift
away from early attempts at social realism and moderate expressionism in
favor of imaginative conceptions, often stimulated by techniques of surrealist
automatism, which gradually paved the way during the 1940s and early 1950s
for his growing commitment to abstraction. Mildly mythological or totemic

figures followed by varieties of symbolic notations witness his search for new subject matter; at the same time references to naturalistic space submit to an increasing flatness. By 1953 Louis's process of distillation yielded two apparently conflicting vocabularies: a cerebral geometric structure and a subjective, free-form imagery.

Louis's conflict obviously parallels in significant respects that of his 1963 audience, who would perhaps not have been so troubled by the apparent dichotomy in his paintings had they been aware of his previous work. The primary reason for their ignorance resulted from the fact that Louis worked and lived in Baltimore and Washington, D.C., not in New York City, and that his work was basically unknown, unexhibited, and, in many respects, unimportant for nearly twenty years. For reasons that are clear in retrospect, his location probably both impeded and fostered his eventual achievement.

Louis's departure from New York about 1944–45 robbed him of the immediate experience of the exceptionally productive and stimulating decade that witnessed radical change in both American painting and in the very nature of the art world. While he may have seen a few important exhibitions in New York on infrequent visits there, and he may have read some of the same books or magazines that circulated among artists' studios, he clearly did not participate in the daily ferment that gave rise to the New York school. He never shared in the studio and bar conversations, nor visited galleries or museums on a regular basis, nor heard the lectures and symposia — formal and informal — that both contributed to and reflected the maturation of abstract expressionism. Even if he had remained in New York City, he probably would not have been a participant in these activities, for with the exception of his friendships with Charles Schucker and Kenneth Noland, Louis was a "loner," too caught up in his work to leave his studio for any but the most compelling reasons.

His position as distant observer rather than active participant in the burgeoning New York school must account, in part, for the subdued overtones rather than immediate intensities of early abstract expressionism in his early work. A similar distinctness of tone characterizes the difference between his mature Veil paintings and the mature paintings of such men as Pollock and Rothko. Clement Greenberg observed in 1960 that distance from New York was important for both Louis and Noland; in fact, unlike Noland, who moved to New York in 1960, Louis was removed from the mainstream for the entirety of his mature career. It is certainly not impossible for an artist to create major innovative work without direct contact with a major cultural center, but it is extremely uncommon. Louis was no exception, for it was only after 1953, when he experienced on a sporadic but consistent basis the stimuli, pressures, and challenges of New York, that he developed the potential of his previous work. Geographical distance may have delayed his maturation, but it also probably saved him from the pitfalls of derivation and provided his passage to innovation. In addition, it must be noted that it was only beginning in 1953 that Louis was able to work in the privacy and security of his own studio in his own home, to afford materials on a relatively consistent basis, and to enjoy positive public response to his paintings.

Without the substantial achievement of Louis's mature paintings, it is unlikely that his drawings would represent more than an interesting footnote to the history of American art. Viewed in conjunction with his paintings, however, the drawings clarify the origins of the problems he confronted during the final eight years of his career. The conflict that emerged in his 1953 drawings continued to haunt him for the rest of the decade, although its terms were altered by the translation to large scale and increasingly bold coloration. Nonetheless, with the exception of his Veil paintings (which occupied him for only eighteen months of the decade), Louis struggled to find a viable structure to contain the freedom and boldness of his expressionist urges.[67] Only in 1960, when he created his supremely innovative Unfurled paintings, was the issue resolved. With the evidence of his drawings now made available to us, it is not surprising to discover that the Unfurled solution evolved from his realization that personal draftsmanship could be used to channel vibrant color into taut compositions in which implied—but not restrictive—geometry intensified rather than opposed the emotional, subjective experience of space and color.

This exhibition and catalogue of Morris Louis's drawings prove that the long-held view that his career "began" in 1954 is severely truncated. This may be the most dramatic example of such historical shortsightedness, but it is not unique. Many of Louis's contemporaries repudiated their early work, believing that it somehow clouded the achievement of their later years; these artists (like others before them) often concealed or destroyed any examples of their early work that had remained in their possession. Only recently has the propagandistic fervor that accompanied the "triumph" of American painting begun to yield to a more balanced historical perspective. With the publication of the Pollock catalogue raisonné, the anticipation of a similar catalogue for Gorky's work, the settlement of the Rothko dispute and resulting freeing of the work for exhibitions like the recent retrospective, the establishment of a Gottlieb foundation, and the example of exhibitions like the Whitney Museum's "Abstract Expressionism: The Formative Years," we can look forward to a thorough examination of the period's major figures. While the conclusions may be neither as dramatic nor as romantic as those characteristic of the previous literature, they are likely to bring us closer to the true nature of the period's achievement.

NOTES

1. Earlier publications on Louis are incorrect in stating that he left the institute before completing the course.

2. "The Cones," in *Handbook of the Cone Collection* (Baltimore: Baltimore Museum of Art, 1955), p. 11.

3. Barbara Pollack, *The Collectors: Dr. Claribel and Miss Etta Cone* (New York, 1962), p. 133.

4. This incident is reported by Pollack, p. 180.

5. Charles Schucker was interviewed on tape by Dr. Anita Faatz on November 18, 1970. The tape has been given to the Archives of American Art by Marcella Louis Brenner; both she and Mr. Schucker granted me permission to use it. In addition, I interviewed Mr. Schucker on June 23, 1978. Unless otherwise noted, the information about the period of the Louis-Schucker friendship comes from these sources.

6. The two were "virtually inseparable companions," according to Chet LaMore, an artist who knew them at the time. In fact, he acknowledged that they were jokingly referred to as the "Gold Dust Twins" (Chet LaMore, letter to the author, August 27, 1978).

7. Mervin Jules, another student at the Maryland Institute of Art during this period, also recalls discussing Cézanne's work with Louis (interview with the author, October 12, 1978).

8. The teacher was Charles Walther, a landscape painter who was fired in 1929. The president of the Maryland Institute's Board of Directors "specifically refused to say that Mr. Walther was dismissed because he didn't draw trees as they actually were in Nature," according to a *Baltimore Sun* interview reported by Pollack, p. 222. The incident was the subject of a *Sun* editorial, in which Walther was supported, and of a pamphlet prepared by Dr. Boas (see Pollack, p. 223).

9. Schucker's recollection of Miss Cone's behavior is supported by Adelyn Breeskin's account of Etta's absolute inability to refuse to give personal tours of the collection, an activity that afforded her great pleasure (interview with the author, October 17, 1978). Etta Cone was interested in some Baltimore artists, including Herman Maril, Aaron Sopher, and Edward Rosenfield, according to Pollack, p. 236.

10. This was the same traveling scholarship previously won by Shelby Shackelford. According to Mervin Jules, the chance to win this scholarship was one of the few things that kept those students with avant-garde tendencies enrolled in the Maryland Institute of Art (interview with the author, October 12, 1978).

11. In addition to the assistance provided by Mrs. Blum, I gratefully acknowledge the information about the mural provided me by Brenda Richardson, assistant director for Art and curator of Painting and Sculpture of the Baltimore Museum, and Judy Sobol, former chairman of the museum's Division of Education.

12. Sam Swerdloff, telephone conversation with the author, August 21, 1978. I am also extremely grateful to Francis V. O'Connor, who provided me with a copy of the PWAP report and offered assistance in locating Louis's WPA records.

13. Francis V. O'Connor, *Federal Support for the Visual Arts: The New Deal and Now* (Greenwich, Conn.: New York Graphic Society, 1969), p. 19.

14. Sam Swerdloff, interview with the author, November 30, 1978. The following information about the mural commission was provided in the interview. I examined and photographed the panels of the mural on November 16, 1978.

15. Mr Swerdloff believes that the studies were exhibited at the Corcoran, but the exhibition catalogue contains no listing that corresponds to this project. The exhibition was viewed by its organizers as an essential forum for stimulating the interest and support of Congress for federally sponsored art projects.

16. Jules, interview with the author.

17. This résumé, which was used by Angelica Rudenstine to prepare a detailed chronology of Louis's career, has unfortunately been lost or misplaced in the Louis estate archives and I was unable to consult it. See Angelica Rudenstine, "Chronology," in *Morris Louis 1912–1962* (Boston: Museum of Fine Arts, 1967), pp. 25–28, and reprinted in Michael Fried, *Morris Louis* (New York: Abrams, 1970).

18. LaMore believes that Louis first contacted him in New York either late in 1937 or early in 1938 (letter to the author, August 27, 1978). Schucker's recollections, however, and Louis's claim that he participated in the Siqueiros Workshop, discussed later in the text, suggest 1936 as the year Louis arrived in New York.

19. LaMore, letter to the author.

20. Leonard Bocour, interview with the author, January 25, 1974, and August 16, 1978.

21. Laurence P. Hurlburt, "The Siqueiros Experimental Workshop: New York 1936," *Art Journal* (Spring 1976): 245.

22. Harold Lehman, "For an Artists' Union Workshop," *Art Front* (October 1937), quoted by Hurlburt, p. 245.

23. Kenworth Moffett, "Noland," *Art International* (Summer 1973): 22. In his monograph on Noland, Mr. Moffett details some of the techniques the two explored together (see Kenworth Moffett, *Kenneth Noland* [New York: Abrams, 1977], p. 40).

24. J. S., "Exhibitions," *Art Front* (March 1937): 16. I would like to thank Brian Wallis for initially bringing this review to my attention.

25. John Lonergan (1895–1969) was probably the supervisor to whom Louis reported, since Lonergan, a supervisor on the Easel Project, was one of the few people Louis claimed to have known in New York during the 1930s.

26. See Joseph Solman, "The Easel Division of the WPA Federal Art Project," in Francis V. O'Connor, ed., *The New Deal Art Projects: An Anthology of Memoirs* (Washington, D.C.: Smithsonian Institution Press, 1972).

27. Morris Louis, letter to Joseph Bernstein, October 31, 1941, Louis estate archives.

28. Stanley Blumberg, a writer who was friendly with Louis and other artists in Baltimore at that time, expressed this sentiment in an interview with the author on November 15, 1978. It was echoed by Louis's other friends who were interviewed.

29. Stephens Berge, letter to the author, January 25, 1978. Herman Maril finds the figure more a likeness of Louis than Berge (interview with the author, November 15, 1978).

30. Although, according to his widow's recollection, Louis was proud of having exhibited at the fair and hung this picture in their home in an unusually elaborate frame. There it remained for the rest of his life as a reminder. I have been unable to confirm his participation in the exhibition at the fair. No work by Louis, for example, is listed in the catalogue for *American Art Today,* the major exhibition of painting at the New York World's Fair in 1939.

31. Henry Geldzahler, *American Painting in the Twentieth Century* (New York: Metropolitan Museum of Art, 1965), pp. 57-59.

32. Leon Berkowitz, interview with the author, August 16, 1975.

33. The jury for the 1949 Maryland artists show, which included among its members James Johnson Sweeney and Jack Tworkov, awarded a prize to Louis's *Sub-Marine* (1948; see p. 56), a picture he showed again later that year in the Corcoran Gallery's "Annual Area Exhibition." In the 1950 Baltimore Museum exhibition, Louis's collage *Nest* won a prize designated "for a work in any medium showing original work in a modern direction."

34. The first students were Dr. Gus Highstein, Lila Katzen, and Helen Jacobson. For the latter's recollections of Louis as a teacher see Helen Jacobson, "As I remember Morris Louis," in *Ten Washington Artists 1950–1970* (Edmonton, Canada: The Edmonton Art Gallery, 1970).

35. In 1957 Louis gave Sawyer a painting that had been exhibited in his one-man show at the Martha Jackson Gallery in New York. Since the picture was too large for Sawyer to hang in his home, he arranged to have it shown at the Baltimore Museum. This led to the mistaken belief on the part of later writers that the museum had acquired the painting. It was later purchased from Sawyer by Vincent Melzac and is now on loan to the National Collection of Fine Arts in Washington.

36. Leonard Bocour recalls a Washington visit when Louis refused to leave his 2½-hour class until it was over, despite Bocour's assurance that it was common practice for studio instructors to be present just long enough to provide critiques (interview with the author, August 16, 1978).

37. Kenneth Noland, interview with Paul Cummings, December 9, 1971, Archives of American Art, p. 17, as quoted in Moffett, *Kenneth Noland,* pp. 20–21.

38. Gene Davis, interview with Barbara Rose, *Artforum* (March 1971), reprinted in Donald Wall, ed., *Gene Davis* (New York: Praeger, 1975), p. 151. Recently, Davis further commented: "I learned later from Leon that faculty members had been called on to volunteer on a particular day to help paint the workshop interior and that Louis was the only one to show up" (Gene Davis, "Starting Out in the '50s," *Art in America* [July–August 1978], p. 90). The two later meetings between Davis and Louis are discussed in an interview with Davis conducted by Walter Hopps, which is reprinted in Wall, p. 122.

39. During the period from 1947 to 1953 major exhibitions at the Phillips Collection included one-man shows of Pierre Bonnard and Karl

Knaths (1952), Nicholas de Staël and Milton Avery (1953), and the Katherine Dreier collection (1953). Significant among new acquisitions were works by Mark Tobey (1947), Joan Miró (1948), Theodoros Stamos (1949, 1950), as well as Avery, Willem de Kooning, Adolph Gottlieb, and Kenneth Noland (all 1952). In 1963 the Phillips acquired Louis's Stripe painting *No. 182,* 1961, which had been exhibited in the Corcoran's Twenty-eighth Biennial; this purchase made the Phillips the first museum to acquire a Louis.

For the best general history that traces the emergence of Washington as a significant provincial art center, see Barbara Rose, "Retrospective Notes on the Washington School," in *The Vincent Melzac Collection* (Washington, D.C.: Corcoran Gallery of Art, 1971).

40. Leslie Judd Portner, "The Workshop and the Watkins," *Washington Post,* February 1, 1953, p. L-5. This is only the first of many articles that linked Louis and Noland together without an acknowledgment of their age difference. At age forty-one, Louis was probably not pleased to be labeled a "young artist," a term more appropriate for the twenty-nine-year-old Noland.

41. Leslie Judd Portner, "One a Newcomer, One a Veteran," *Washington Post,* April 12, 1953, p. L-3.

42. Gladys Harrison, "Gallery Gazer," *Times-Herald,* April 26, 1953, p. M5.

43. Rudenstine, "Chronology," p. 26. I have explored the consequences of the New York visit for Louis's career in "In Addition to the Veils," *Art in America* (January–February 1978): 84–94.

44. Louis gave these two drawings to friends as a wedding present in 1953; he showed them two sketchpads and asked them to select one drawing from each (Jeannette Kear, letter to the author, August 14, 1978). The size and type of paper and the nature of the imagery indicate that the drawings were removed from sketchpads number 17 and 18. Some of the drawings found in these two sketchpads were not actually attached pages and are on a different size and type of paper, but their style and imagery are consistent with the attached sheets.

45. That Louis admired *Guernica* is confirmed by a statement he wrote in 1950 in conjunction with a commission for the United States Public Health Service. He discussed the fact that part of the mural's strength resulted from its restriction to black, white, and gray, a color limitation contrary to the viewer's expectations.

46. In 1950 Louis used another device employed by Picasso in the illustrations for the same book when he made drawings in which thin lines connect large dots and form "constellations." Picasso had done similar drawings in 1926 and Vollard included sixteen pages of them, rendered as woodcuts, in the edition of Balzac. Miró's work also includes a similar device. David Smith rendered the same pattern in several of his "Steel Drawings" of 1945.

47. This painting and a set of photographs documenting its various stages were acquired by Etta Cone soon after the painting's completion. This was, however, after the period during which Louis visited the Cone Collection.

48. As far as I know this is the only signed and dated drawing from the 1940s that Louis did not give away to friends. It remained in his estate and was only later given by his widow to her mother. At that time it was removed from sketchpad number 5, a fact determined by the similar spiral binding and by a pattern of tiny worm holes discovered in every page of this sketchpad.

49. See William Rubin, *Miró in the Collection of the Museum of Modern Art* (New York: Museum of Modern Art, 1973), pp. 46–50.

50. Ethel Schwabacher, *Arshile Gorky* (New York: Macmillan, 1957); Harry Rand, *Arshile Gorky: The Implication of Symbols* (Montclair, N.J.: Abner Schram & Co., forthcoming).

51. Louis's arrival in New York was probably too late for him to see the Guild Art Gallery's exhibition "Abstract Drawings by Arshile Gorky," which was held from December 16, 1935, through January 5, 1936, and included eighteen drawings from the "Nighttime Enigma and Nostalgia" series. He might have seen the one drawing from the same series that was acquired by the Société Anonyme during the 1930s. (I am grateful to Jim M. Jordan for providing me with this information.)

52. In fact, prints that explored surrealist automatism were produced, by Pollock among others, in the New York branch of Atelier 17, which Stanley William Hayter directed after he emigrated from Paris in 1940. Atelier 17 received widespread recognition due primarily to the success of a 1944 Museum of Modern Art exhibition that was circulated in this country for two years. Hayter was also deemed sufficiently important by Robert Motherwell and Harold Rosenberg, two of the editors of *Possibilities,* that two of his drawings and a

short essay of his were included in the single issue of the review in the winter of 1947–48. Some of Louis's drawings are similar to Hayter's, whose work he may have known from these sources or, less likely, from Hayter's lecture at the ICA in Washington.

53. See Rosalind Krauss, *Terminal Iron Works: The Sculpture of David Smith* (Cambridge, Mass: MIT Press, 1971), p. 93. About 1953 Noland introduced Louis to Smith, whose work Louis admired and with whom he remained friendly until his own death.

54. It is uncertain precisely how many paintings comprise this series. Four remain in the Louis estate, one belongs to Daniel Millsaps, and another to Leonard Bocour. In addition, Mr. Bocour owns two other closely related pictures; according to him, one is titled *Marcella and Joe Went Walking* and the other is untitled. This last picture, which contains a large, six-pointed star, might be *Man Reaching for a Star,* also exhibited at the Washington Workshop in April 1953.

55. Interview with the author, August 16, 1975.

56. The large, six-pointed Star of David on the picture in the Bocour collection would seem to represent a confirmation of Louis's striking out against Nazi tactics.

57. Louis had at least one other opportunity to see an original Pollock before his trip to New York in 1953. In March and April 1952 the Phillips Collection mounted an exhibition called "Painters of Expressionist Abstractions," which included Pollock's *Number 24,* (1950). Although Francis O'Connor was unable to locate the picture when preparing the Pollock catalogue raisonné, Gene Davis described it to him as a "baby brother to such paintings as *Lavender Mist*" (see Francis Valentine O'Connor and Eugene Victor Thaw, eds., *Jackson Pollock: A Catalogue Raisonné of Paintings, Drawings, and Other Works* [New Haven, Conn.: Yale University Press, 1978], catalogue #313).

58. Michael Fried, conversation with the author, November 28, 1978.

59. B. H. Friedman, *Jackson Pollock: Energy Made Visible* (New York: McGraw Hill, 1972), p. 92.

60. At about the same time Louis executed designs that used similar formal devices for Public Health Service pamphlets about heart disease and hypertension; he was not awarded the commissions.

61. They were partly inspired by several exhibitions at the Museum of Modern Art, including "Prehistoric Rock Pictures in Europe and Africa" (1937), "Twenty Centuries of Mexican Art" (1940), and "Indian Art of the United States" (1941).

62. Lawrence Alloway, "Baziotes: Modern Mythologist," *Art News* (February 1965): 30.

63. These titles were not given by Louis but were apparently suggested to him by Ida Berkowitz (interview with the author, August 16, 1975).

64. D499 and D500 were executed on an unusual paper that is both very heavy and expensive. It is identical to paper used by David Smith during the same period. In addition, the techniques and mediums used by the two artists when working on this paper are identical, as are the resulting conservation problems. Since Louis met Smith in 1953, it seems unlikely that these facts are coincidental. (Marjorie Cohn, associate conservator at the Fogg Art Museum, brought this information to my attention.)

65. Two fake sketches for Unfurleds were reproduced as catalogue numbers 6 and 7 of the *Koelner Kunstmarkt Katalogue* in January 1971. They were withdrawn from sale upon notification by the attorney for the Louis estate.

66. See Daniel Robbins, "Morris Louis at the Juncture of Two Traditions," *Quadrum* (1965): 41–54.

67. This idea is developed at length in the article cited above in note 43.

CATALOGUE OF THE DRAWINGS OF MORRIS LOUIS

The following catalogue documents all the known drawings by Morris Louis. All except ten of the drawings remained in his estate in the form of twenty-five sketchpads and one portfolio of gouaches. Nine drawings, which the original owners acquired from the artist or his widow, are in private collections; and one drawing is now owned by the Maryland Institute, College of Art, Baltimore.

In preparation for the publication of this catalogue and its accompanying exhibition, the sketchpads belonging to the Estate of Morris Louis were dismantled to permit the photographing, exhibition, and proper storage of the individual works. The dismantling of the sketchpads was supervised by Diane Upright Headley. All pages were removed from each sketchpad and numbered in sequence from front to back. In instances where the cover of the pad had been used for a drawing, it was assigned the first number in the group. Sheets with drawings on both sides were assigned a single number with the suffix A given to the recto, and B given to the verso. For example, D188A and D188B represent a single sheet with drawings on both sides. These numbers were not inscribed in every case on the drawings themselves, but do appear beside each drawing in the set of photographs taken for the records of the Estate of Morris Louis.

In five instances drawings not actually belonging to the estate were assigned estate numbers and embossed with the estate seal (see below). They are drawings with the estate numbers D1, D2, D39, D40A and D40B, and D494, which were included with the estate drawings for purposes of photographing, but are all in private collections.

Estate drawings were embossed with a small seal containing the letters ML circumscribed by an oval (ML). This seal appears in the lower right corner of almost every drawing. The exceptions represent instances in which it was later determined that the proper orientation of the drawing differed from that originally perceived, or a few cases in which the drawing was not embossed with the seal. Any variations have been noted in the catalogue entries.

The following chart provides a concordance of the drawings (D1–D503) assigned numbers during photographing. The first column gives the number of the estate sketchpad or portfolio in which the drawing was located. This sketchpad number is an inventory designation and has no other significance. The numbers assigned to the drawings are shown in the second column. The total number of drawings in each sketchpad is indicated in the third column. Drawings on the recto and verso of a single sheet were counted separately. Drawings dated by the artist are indicated in the fourth column. The year is followed by the number of drawings in the sketchpad that bears that date. For example, 2:1953 indicates that two drawings in the sketchpad were dated 1953 by the artist. Certain inconsistencies occurred during the photographing and numbering procedure. Each is explained under the fifth column, Notes, which also includes other pertinent information about the drawings.

SKETCHPAD NUMBER	NUMBERS ASSIGNED TO DRAWINGS	NUMBER OF DRAWINGS IN SKETCHPAD	NUMBER OF DATED DRAWINGS	NOTES
None	D1, D2	2	2:1948	Louis gave these two drawings to their present owner in 1953. Each was selected from a different sketchpad. The size and type of paper and the nature of the imagery suggest that one was removed from sketchpad 17 and the other from sketchpad 18.
2	D3–D27	25	None	This sketchpad was probably used in Florida (see notes for sketchpad 5). The horned animal that appears in several of these drawings also appears in D39, which is dated 1949, a likely date for this group.
3	D28–D38	12	None	The imagery of many of these drawings is quite similar to that of D1 and D2, both of which are dated 1948, a likely date for this group.
None	D39	1	1:1949	See below, notes for sketchpad 5.
None	D40	2	None	See below, notes for sketchpad 1.
None	D41	1	None	See below, notes for sketchpad 7.
1	D42–D46; D204–D214; (D40?)	16 (17?)	2:1953	The break in continuity of numbering resulted from an initial attempt to photograph together drawings from different sketchpads whose imagery was closely related. It was soon perceived that the magnitude of the project made such a task impossible and the plan was abandoned. D40 had been removed from a sketchpad at an earlier date when it was given to its present owner. The size and type of paper and the nature of the imagery strongly suggest that it originally belonged to this sketchpad. Although two of the drawings are dated 1953, some of the pages are very similar to drawings dated 1949. Louis may have used the tablet at two different times, or he may have reworked earlier drawings at a later date.

SKETCHPAD NUMBER	NUMBERS ASSIGNED TO DRAWINGS	NUMBER OF DRAWINGS IN SKETCHPAD	NUMBER OF DATED DRAWINGS	NOTES
17	D47–D65	23	None	This sketchpad probably dates from about 1948, based upon comparison with drawings D1 and D2. Drawings D64 and D65 were loose pages found stored in this pad.
12	D66–D73	10	None	Only D72 was actually attached to this tablet; all others were loose sheets stored in it. Both front and back covers were drawn on. The back cover bears the identifying stamp of a New York art supply store.
18	D74–D118	50	None	D91–D118 were loose pages stored in this sketchpad.
23	D119–D136	18	None	In 1950 Louis was commissioned by the United States Public Health Service (PHS) to design a tuberculosis display. The display was set up at a convention in San Francisco to which Louis accompanied his wife, who was then employed by the PHS. During his visit Louis purchased this sketchpad and sketchpad 26, both of which bear the address of a San Francisco art supply store on their covers. The drawings in both sketchpads are repetitions of a very few different images, most of which related to ideas introduced in the PHS commission designs.
26	D137–D155	19	None	See above, notes for sketchpad 23.
None	D156	1	None	This drawing was selected by Louis to hang in his home.
22	D157–D177	21	None	
25	D178–D186	9	None	
21	D187–D203	34	None	
1	D204–D214	11	2:1953	See above, notes for sketchpad 1.
4	D215–D232	18	11:1953	
5	D233–D248; D39	18	1:1949 1:1953	This sketchpad was purchased in Miami, Florida, as indicated by an art supply store's stamp on its cover. A pattern of tiny holes, apparently caused by worms, was found on each sheet; the number of holes increases from two in the cover and first four pages to eight holes in the last four pages. D39 had been removed from the pad at an earlier date when it was given to its present owner. The presence of two worm holes and holes from the spiral ring binder, both unique to this pad, indicate that D39 belonged to it. These facts were not known at the time of photographing, which accounts for the disparity in numbering. As is the case with sketchpad 1, this pad seems to have been used at two different times.

SKETCHPAD NUMBER	NUMBERS ASSIGNED TO DRAWINGS	NUMBER OF DRAWINGS IN SKETCHPAD	NUMBER OF DATED DRAWINGS	NOTES
6	D250–D260; (D249?)	11 (12?)	7:1953 (8?)	The cover of sketchpad 6 is identical to that of sketchpad 5, although no identifying stamp is present and the spiral ring binder is a different type. It seems likely that sketchpad 6 was also purchased in Miami. D249 had been removed at an earlier date; the holes from the binding and all other aspects indicate that it belonged to this sketchpad.
7	D261–D278; D41	20	8:1953	D41 was found as a loose page stored in this sketchpad. It is not known when it was placed there or who did so. It is possible that Louis was responsible, since its imagery is a likely source for the more freely rendered drawing D262. The disparity in numbering resulted from a decision to photograph and number D41 with a group of stylistically similar works.
8	D279–D288	10	4:1953	
9	D289–D306	18	10:1953	
11	D307–D344	38	None	D335–D344 were found as loose sheets stored in this sketchpad. They are on the same type of tracing paper and display imagery quite similar to those of the attached sheets.
13	D345–D364	20	None	
14	D365–D376	13	None	
15	D377–D396	28	None	D396 is a smaller sheet that was stored in this sketchpad.
16	D397–D412	16	4:1953	
19	D413–D427	16	None	D421–D427 were found as loose sheets stored in this sketchpad.
20	D428–D474	62	1:1953	Only D428–D445 were attached to the sketchpad. All other sheets were loose, with the exception of D454–D460, which constituted a small sketchpad stored in the larger one.
24	D475–D493	19	None	D492 and D493 were found as loose sheets stored in this sketchpad.
None	D494	1	None	This drawing belongs to a private collection; it was photographed and numbered with the estate drawings.
10	D495–D503	10	1:1939 1:1940 1:1941 1:1953	For their protection this group of gouaches was stored in portfolio 10 by Louis's widow.

The catalogue is arranged numerically by estate number, D1 through D503, followed by five drawings, #504 through #508, not numbered by the estate, which are arranged chronologically. The dates that appear in brackets have been assigned to the drawings by Diane Upright Headley. Unless otherwise indicated in the entries, all the drawings are on paper, are unsigned, are owned by the Estate of Morris Louis, and are embossed with the estate seal in the lower right corner. Dimensions are in inches followed by centimeters, height preceding width, and are of the sheet size. In measuring, inches are rounded off to the next highest one-sixteenth of an inch and centimeters are rounded off to the next highest millimeter. The cataloguing of the drawings was done in the Department of Prints and Drawings, National Collection of Fine Arts.

With the exception of D215 *(Geometry of a Fish)* and #504 *(Portrait of Stephens Berge),* the drawings are untitled.

D1. Pen and ink on paperboard   1948
13⅞ x 16⅝ (35.1 x 42.1)
Signed lower right in pencil: M. Louis 48
Jeannette F. Kear, Chevy Chase, Maryland

D3. Pen and ink   [1949]
18¹³/₁₆ x 23⅞ (47.7 x 60.7)

D5. Pen and ink   [1949]
18¾ x 23¹³/₁₆ (47.6 x 60.5)

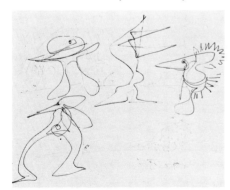

D2. Pen and ink on paperboard   1948
13¹³/₁₆ x 16¾ (35.0 x 42.4)
Signed lower right in pencil: M Louis –48
Jeannette F. Kear, Chevy Chase, Maryland

D4. Pen and ink   [1949]
18¹³/₁₆ x 23⅞ (47.7 x 60.5)

D6. Pen and ink   [1949]
18¾ x 23⅞ (47.6 x 60.5)

D7. Pen and ink   [1949]
18¾ x 23¹³/₁₆ (47.6 x 60.5)

D10. Pen and ink   [1949]
18¾ x 23¹³/₁₆ (47.6 x 60.5)

D13. Pen and ink   [1949]
18¹³/₁₆ x 23¹³/₁₆ (47.6 x 60.5)

D8. Pen and ink   [1949]
18¾ x 23¹³/₁₆ (47.6 x 60.5)

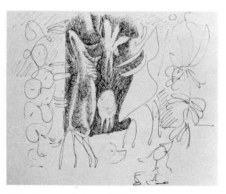

D11. Pen and ink   [1949]
18¹³/₁₆ x 23⅞ (47.7 x 60.5)

D14. Pen and ink   [1949]
18¹³/₁₆ x 23¹³/₁₆ (47.7 x 60.5)

D9. Pen and ink   [1949]
18¾ x 23¹³/₁₆ (47.6 x 60.5)

D12. Pen and ink   [1949]
18¹³/₁₆ 23¹³/₁₆ (47.7 x 60.5)

D15. Pen and ink   [1949]
18¹³/₁₆ x 23¹³/₁₆ (47.6 x 60.4)

D16. Pen and ink   [1949]
18¹³/₁₆ x 23¹³/₁₆ (47.6 x 60.4)

D17. Pen and ink   [1949]
18¾ x 23¹³/₁₆ (47.6 x 60.5)

D18. Pen and ink   [1949]
23¹³/₁₆ x 18¾ (60.5 x 47.6)

D19. Pen and ink   [1949]
23¹³/₁₆ x 18¾ (60.5 x 47.6)

D20. Pen and ink   [1949]
23¹³/₁₆ x 18¾ (60.5 x 47.6)

D21. Pen and ink   [1949]
18¾ x 23¹³/₁₆ (47.6 x 60.5)
No estate seal

D22. Pen and ink   [1949]
18¾ x 23¹³/₁₆ (47.6 x 60.5)

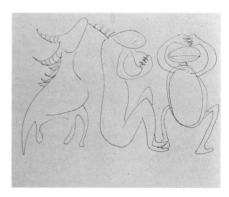

D23. Pen and ink   [1949]
18¾ x 23⅞ (47.6 x 60.5)

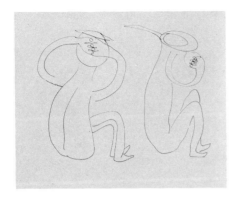

D24. Pen and ink   [1949]
18¾ x 23⅞ (47.6 x 60.5)

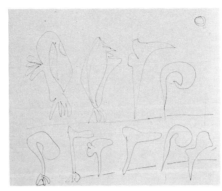

D27. Pen and ink   [1949]
18¾ x 23¹³⁄₁₆ (47.6 x 60.4)

D29B. Pen and ink   [1948]
18¾ x 23¹³⁄₁₆ (47.6 x 60.4)
Estate seal embossed lower left in reverse

D25. Pen and ink   [1949]
18¾ x 23¹³⁄₁₆ (47.6 x 60.5)

D28. Pen and ink   [1948]
18¾ x 23¹³⁄₁₆ (47.6 x 60.4)

D30. Pen and ink   [1948]
18¾ x 23¹³⁄₁₆ (47.6 x 60.4)

D26. Pen and ink   [1949]
18¾ x 23¹³⁄₁₆ (47.6 x 60.5)

D29A. Pen and ink   [1948]
18¾ x 23¹³⁄₁₆ (47.6 x 60.4)

D31. Pen and ink   [1948]
18¾ x 23¹³⁄₁₆ (47.6 x 60.4)

D32. Pen and ink   [1948]
18¾ x 23¹³/₁₆ (47.6 x 60.4)

D35. Pen and ink   [1948]
18¾ x 23¹³/₁₆ (47.6 x 60.4)

D38. Pen and ink   [1948]
18¾ x 23¹³/₁₆ (47.6 x 60.4)

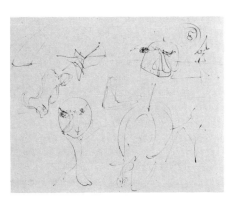

D33. Pen and ink   [1948]
18¾ x 23¹³/₁₆ (47.6 x 60.4)

D36. Pen and ink   [1948]
18¾ x 23¹³/₁₆ (47.6 x 60.4)

D39. Pen and ink   1949
18⅝ x 23⅝ (47.2 x 60.0)
Signed lower right in ink: Louis 49
Mrs. Moses Siegel, Washington, D. C.

D34. Pen and ink   [1948]
18¾ x 23¹³/₁₆ (47.6 x 60.4)

D37. Pen and ink   [1948]
18¾ x 23¹³/₁₆ (47.6 x 60.4)

D40A. Pen and ink   [1949]
18½ x 23¹³/₁₆ (46.9 x 60.4)
Mrs. Moses Siegel, Washington, D. C.

D40B. Pen and ink   [1949]
18½ x 23¹³/₁₆ (46.9 x 60.4)
Estate seal embossed lower left in reverse
Mrs. Moses Siegel, Washington, D.C.

D43. Pen and ink   [1949]
18¾ x 23¹³/₁₆ (47.6 x 60.4)

D46. Pen and ink   [1949]
18¾ x 23¹³/₁₆ (47.6 x 60.4)

D41. Pen and ink   [1949]
18¾ x 23¹³/₁₆ (47.6 x 60.4)

D44. Pen and ink   [1949]
18¾ x 23¹³/₁₆ (47.6 x 60.4)

D47. Pen and ink   [1948]
13⅝ x 16¹¹/₁₆ (34.4 x 42.3)

D42. Pen and ink   [1949]
18¾ x 23¹³/₁₆ (47.6 x 60.4)

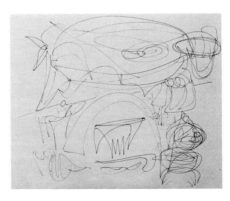

D45. Pen and ink   [1949]
18¾ x 23¹³/₁₆ (47.6 x 60.4)

D48. Pen and ink   [1948]
13¹⁵/₁₆ x 16¾ (35.4 x 42.5)

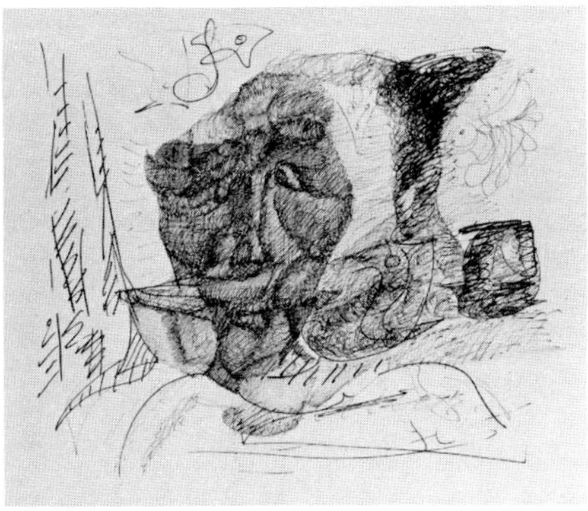

D49A. Pen and ink [1948]
13 5/8 x 16 11/16 (34.5 x 42.3)

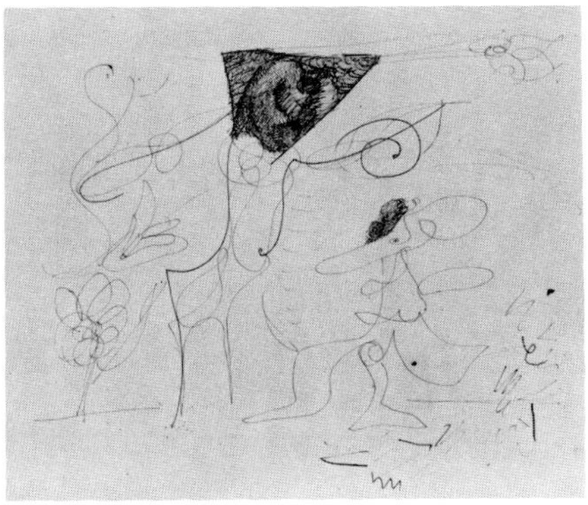

D49B. Pen and ink [1948]
13 5/8 x 16 11/16 (34.5 x 42.3)
Estate seal embossed lower left in reverse

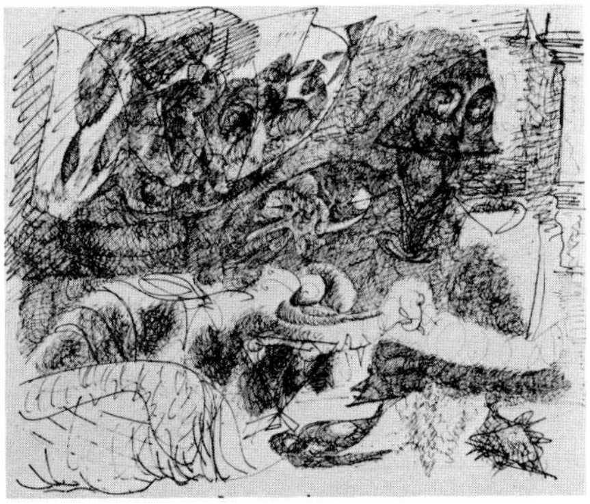

D50. Pen and ink [1948]
13 5/8 x 16 11/16 (34.5 x 42.3)

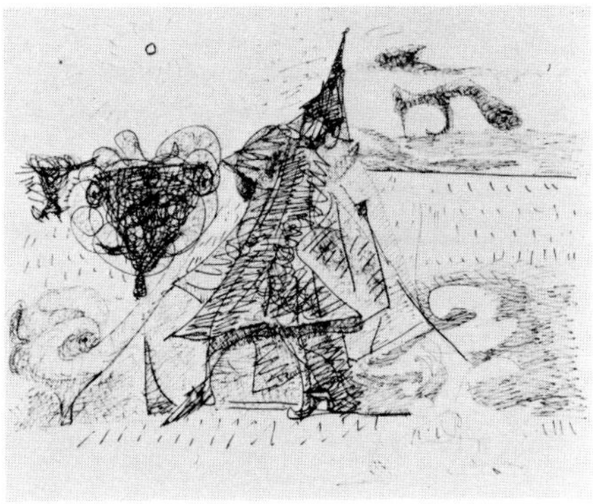

D51A. Pen and ink [1948]
13 5/8 x 16 11/16 (34.5 x 42.3)

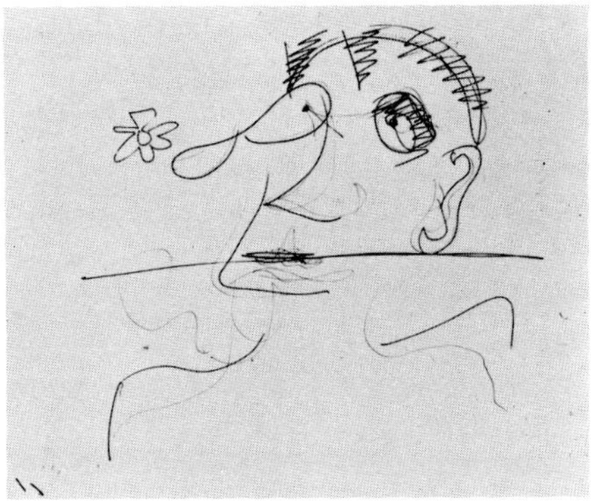

D51B. Pen and ink [1948]
13 5/8 x 16 11/16 (34.5 x 42.3)
Estate seal embossed lower left in reverse

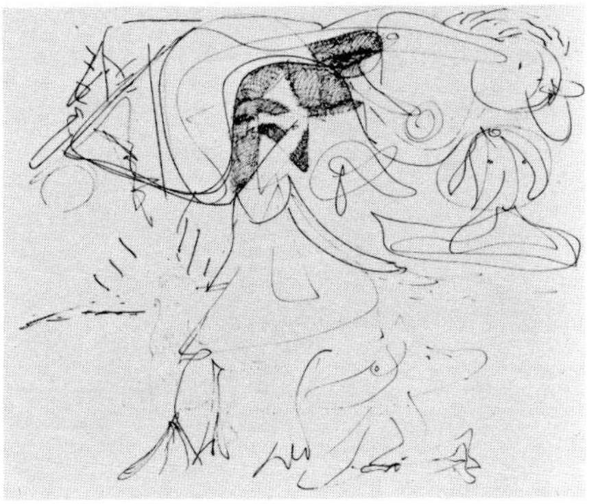

D52. Pen and ink [1948]
13 15/16 x 16 3/4 (35.3 x 42.4)

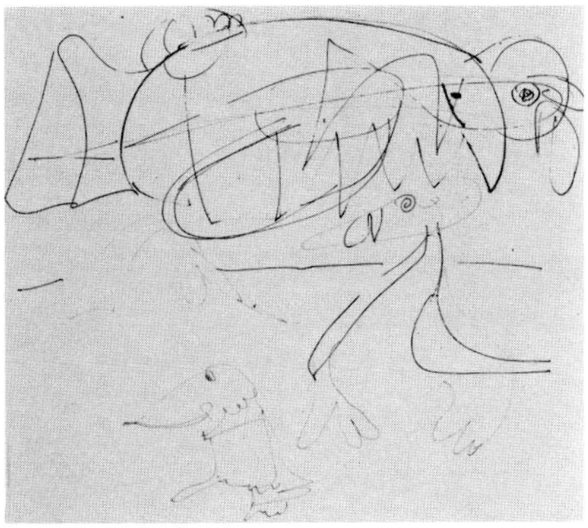

D53. Pen and ink [1948]
13 15/16 x 16 3/4 (35.3 x 42.4)

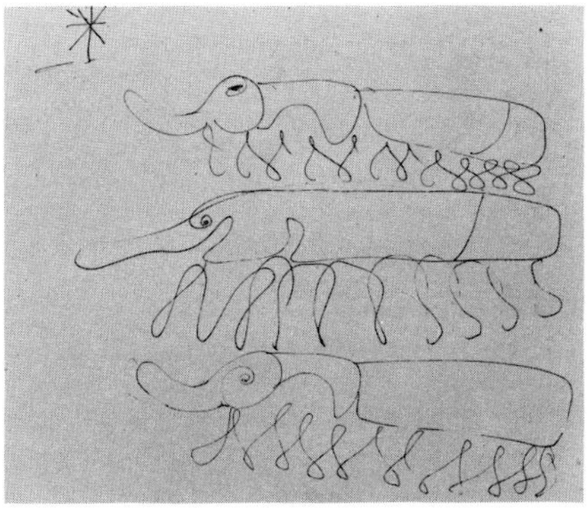

D54. Pen and ink [1948]
13 15/16 x 16 11/16 (35.3 x 42.4)

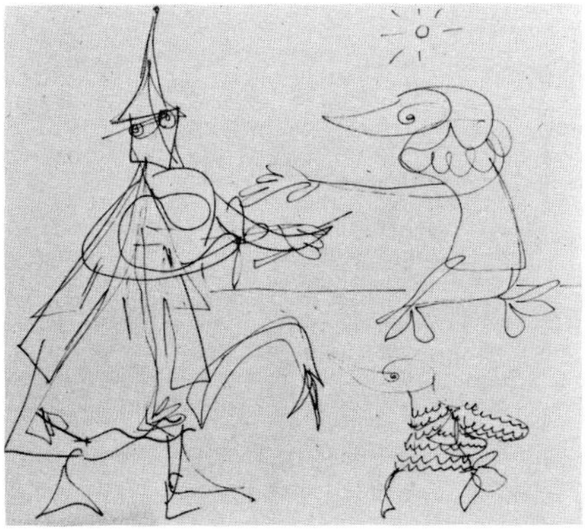

D55. Pen and ink [1948]
13 15/16 x 16 3/4 (35.3 x 42.4)

D56. Pen and ink   [1948]
13¹⁵/₁₆ x 16¾ (35.3 x 42.4)

D59. Pen and ink   [1948]
13¹⁵/₁₆ x 16¾ (35.3 x 42.4)

D61. Pen and ink   [1948]
13¹⁵/₁₆ x 16¾ (35.3 x 42.4)

D57. Pen and ink   [1948]
13¹⁵/₁₆ x 16¾ (35.3 x 42.4)

D60A. Pen and ink   [1948]
13¹⁵/₁₆ x 16¾ (35.3 x 42.4)

D62. Pen and ink   [1948]
13¹⁵/₁₆ x 16¹¹/₁₆ (35.3 x 42.4)

D58. Pen and ink   [1948]
13¹⁵/₁₆ x 16¹¹/₁₆ (35.3 x 42.4)

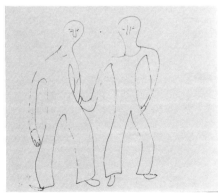

D60B. Pen and ink   [1948]
13¹⁵/₁₆ x 16¾ (35.3 x 42.4)
Estate seal embossed lower left in reverse

D63. Pen and ink   [1948]
13¹⁵/₁₆ x 16¹¹/₁₆ (35.3 x 42.4)

D64A. Pen and ink   [1948]
8¹¹/₁₆ x 11¾ (22.1 x 29.7)

D66A. Pencil and pen and ink with touches
of gouache   [1948]
11 x 13¹³/₁₆ (27.9 x 35.0)

D67. Pen and ink with touches of
gouache   [1948]
irregular: 11¹/₁₆ x 7⁹/₁₆ (28.0 x 19.2)

D64B. Pen and ink   [1948]
8¹¹/₁₆ x 11¾ (22.1 x 29.7)
Estate seal embossed lower left in reverse

D66B. Pencil with touches of ink   [1948]
13¹³/₁₆ x 11 (35.0 x 27.9)
Estate seal embossed upper left in reverse

D68A. Pen and ink   [1948]
irregular: 11¹/₁₆ x 13⅝ (28.0 x 34.6)

D65. Pen and ink   [1948]
12¹/₁₆ x 15¹⁵/₁₆ (30.6 x 40.4)

D68B. Pen and ink [1948]
irregular: 11¹/₁₆ x 13⁵/₈ (28.0 x 34.6)
Estate seal embossed lower left in reverse

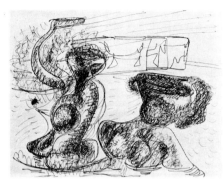

D70. Pen and ink [1948]
12¹/₁₆ x 15¹⁵/₁₆ (30.6 x 40.4)

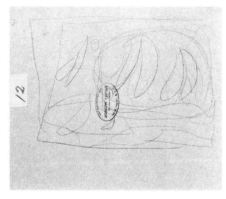

D73. Pencil and stamped ink on
paperboard [1948]
11 x 13¾ (27.9 x 34.9)

D69. Pen and ink [1948]
15¹⁵/₁₆ x 12¹/₁₆ (40.4 x 30.6)

D71. Pen and ink [1948]
12¹/₁₆ x 15¹⁵/₁₆ (30.6 x 40.4)

D74. Pen and ink and pencil [1948]
13⁵/₈ x 16¹¹/₁₆ (34.5 x 42.3)

D72. Pen and ink [1948]
11¹/₁₆ x 13¹³/₁₆ (28.0 x 35.0)

D75. Pen and ink [1948]
13⁵/₈ x 16¹¹/₁₆ (34.5 x 42.3)

D76. Pen and ink   [1948]
14 x 16⅞ (35.3 x 42.7)

D78. Pen and ink   [1948]
16¹³/₁₆ x 14 (42.7 x 35.5)

D80. Pen and ink   [1948]
16¹³/₁₆ x 14 (42.7 x 35.4)

D77. Pen and ink   [1948]
14 x 16¹³/₁₆ (35.5 x 42.7)

D81. Pen and ink   [1948]
13⅝ x 16¹¹/₁₆ (34.5 x 42.3)

D79. Pen and ink   [1948]
16¹³/₁₆ x 14 (42.7 x 35.5)

D82. Pen and ink   [1948]
13⅝ x 16¹¹/₁₆ (34.5 x 42.3)

D85. Pen and ink   [1948]
13⅝ x 16¹¹/₁₆ (34.5 x 42.3)

D88. Pen and ink   [1948]
13⅝ x 16¹¹/₁₆ (34.5 x 42.3)

D83. Pen and ink   [1948]
13⅝ x 16¹¹/₁₆ (34.5 x 42.3)

D86. Pen and ink   [1948]
13⅝ x 16¹¹/₁₆ (34.5 x 42.3)

D89. Pen and ink   [1948]
13⅝ x 16¹¹/₁₆ (34.5 x 42.3)

D84. Pen and ink   [1948]
13⅝ x 16¹¹/₁₆ (34.5 x 42.3)

D87. Pen and ink   [1948]
13⅝ x 16¹¹/₁₆ (34.5 x 42.3)

D90. Pen and ink   [1948]
13⅝ x 16¹¹/₁₆ (34.5 x 42.3)

D91. Pen and ink   [1948]
14⁷⁄₈ x 11¹³⁄₁₆ (37.7 x 30.0)

D92B. Pen and ink   [1948]
irregular: 13¹³⁄₁₆ x 11¹⁄₁₆ (35.0 x 28.0)
Estate seal embossed lower right in reverse

D94. Pen and ink   [1948]
11¹⁄₁₆ x 13¹³⁄₁₆ (28.0 x 35.0)

D92A. Pen and ink   [1948]
irregular: 11¹⁄₁₆ x 13¹³⁄₁₆ (28.0 x 35.0)

D93. Pen and ink   [1948]
irregular: 11¹⁄₁₆ x 13¹³⁄₁₆ (28.0 x 35.0)

D95. Pen and ink   [1948]
11¹⁄₁₆ x 13¹³⁄₁₆ (28.0 x 35.0)
No estate seal

D96. Pen and ink and pencil   [1948]
11¹³⁄₁₆ x 14⁷⁄₈ (30.0 x 37.7)

D97A. Pen and ink   [1948]
11¹/₁₆ x 13¹³/₁₆ (28.0 x 35.0)

D99A. Pen and ink   [1948]
11¹/₁₆ x 13¹³/₁₆ (28.0 x 35.0)
No estate seal

D100. Pen and ink   [1948]
11¹/₁₆ x 13¹³/₁₆ (28.0 x 35.0)

D97B. Pen and ink   [1948]
11¹/₁₆ x 13¹³/₁₆ (28.0 x 35.0)
Estate seal embossed lower left in reverse

D101. Pen and ink   [1948]
11¹/₁₆ x 13¹³/₁₆ (28.0 x 35.0)

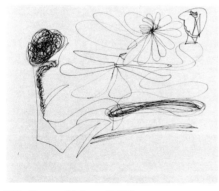

D98. Pen and ink   [1948]
11¹/₁₆ x 13¹³/₁₆ (28.0 x 35.0)

D99B. Pen and ink   [1948]
13¹³/₁₆ x 11¹/₁₆ (35.0 x 28.0)
No estate seal

D102. Pen and ink   [1948]
irregular: 11⅞ x 16¹/₁₆ (30.1 x 40.7)

D103. Pen and ink [1948]
11⁷⁄₈ x 16¹⁄₁₆ (30.1 x 40.7)

D105. Pen and ink [1948]
11⁷⁄₈ x 16¹⁄₁₆ (30.1 x 40.7)

D107. Pen and ink [1948]
14¹⁄₄ x 10⁷⁄₈ (36.2 x 27.6)

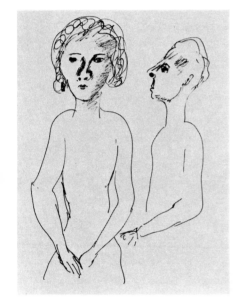

D104. Pen and ink [1948]
16¹⁄₁₆ x 11⁷⁄₈ (40.7 x 30.1)
Estate seal embossed lower left

D106. Pen and ink [1948]
11⁷⁄₈ x 16¹⁄₁₆ (30.1 x 40.7)

D108. Pen and ink and pencil [1948]
16 x 12¹⁄₈ (40.7 x 30.7)

D109. Pen and ink   [1948]
12¹/₁₆ x 15¹⁵/₁₆ (30.6 x 40.4)

D112. Pen and ink   [1948]
8¹¹/₁₆ x 11¾ (22.0 x 29.7)

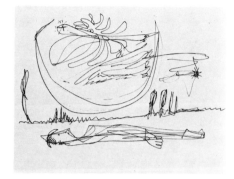

D114. Pen and ink   [1948]
8¹¹/₁₆ x 11¾ (22.1 x 29.8)

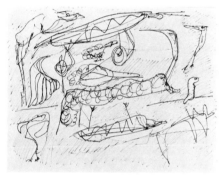

D110. Pen and ink   [1948]
8¹¹/₁₆ x 11¾ (22.1 x 29.7)

D113A. Pen and ink   [1948]
8¹¹/₁₆ x 11¾ (22.1 x 29.8)

D115. Pen and ink   [1948]
8¹¹/₁₆ x 11¾ (22.0 x 29.7)

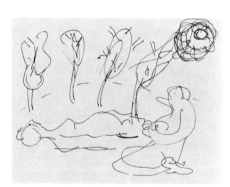

D111. Pen and ink   [1948]
8¹¹/₁₆ x 11¾ (22.0 x 29.7)

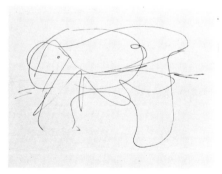

D113B. Pen and ink   [1948]
8¹¹/₁₆ x 11¾ (22.1 x 29.8)
Estate seal embossed lower left in reverse

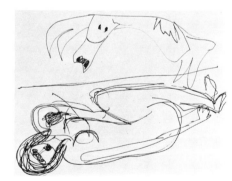

D116A. Pen and ink   [1948]
8¹¹/₁₆ x 11¾ (22.1 x 29.7)

D116B. Pen and ink   [1948]
8¹¹/₁₆ x 11¾ (22.1 x 29.7)
Estate seal embossed upper right in reverse

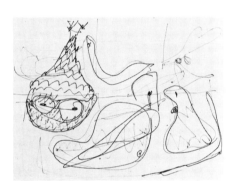

D117. Pen and ink   [1948]
8¹¹/₁₆ x 11¾ (22.0 x 29.7)

D118. Pen and ink   [1950]
11¹⁵/₁₆ x 8⅞ (30.2 x 22.6)

D119. Pen and ink   [1950]
11 x 13⅞ (27.9 x 35.1)

D120. Pen and ink   [1950]
11 x 13⅞ (27.9 x 35.1)

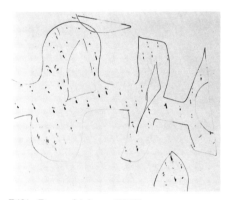

D121. Pen and ink   [1950]
11 x 13⅞ (27.9 x 35.1)

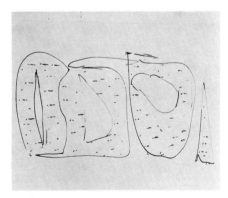

D122. Pen and ink   [1950]
11 x 13⅞ (27.9 x 35.1)

D123. Pen and ink   [1950]
11 x 13⅞ (27.9 x 35.1)

D126. Pen and ink   [1950]
11 x 13⅞ (27.9 x 35.1)

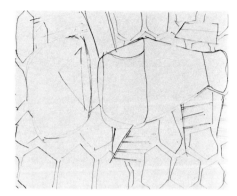

D129. Pen and ink   [1950]
11 x 13⅞ (27.9 x 35.1)

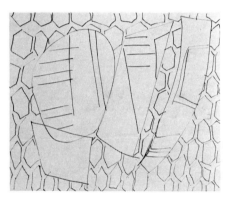

D124. Pen and ink   [1950]
11 x 13⅞ (27.9 x 35.1)

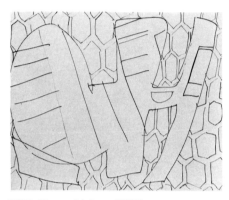

D127. Pen and ink   [1950]
11 x 13¹³/₁₆ (27.9 x 35.1)

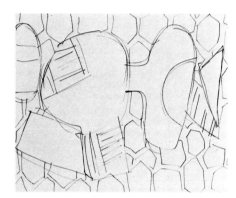

D130. Pen and ink   [1950]
11 x 13⅞ (27.9 x 35.1)

D125. Pen and ink   [1950]
11 x 13¹³/₁₆ (27.9 x 35.1)

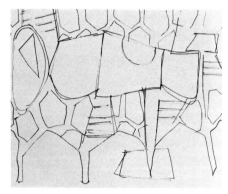

D128. Pen and ink   [1950]
11 x 13⅞ (27.9 x 35.1)

D131. Pen and ink   [1950]
11 x 13¹³/₁₆ (27.9 x 35.1)

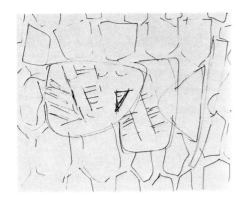

D132. Pen and ink [1950]
11 x 13⅞ (27.9 x 35.1)

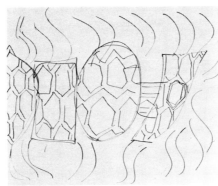

D135. Pen and ink [1950]
11 x 13⅞ (27.9 x 35.1)

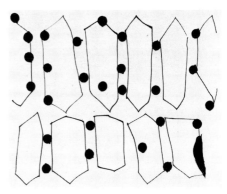

D138. Pen and ink, and brush and ink [1950]
11¹/₁₆ x 13⅞ (28.0 x 35.1)

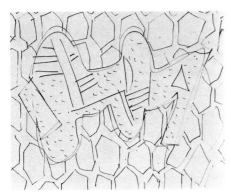

D133. Pen and ink [1950]
11 x 13¹³/₁₆ (27.9 x 35.1)

D136. Pen and ink [1950]
11 x 13⅞ (27.9 x 35.1)

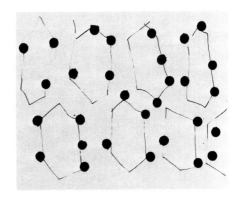

D139. Pen and ink, and brush and ink [1950]
11¹/₁₆ x 13⅞ (28.0 x 35.1)

D134. Pen and ink [1950]
11 x 13⅞ (27.9 x 35.1)

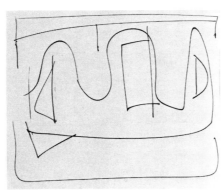

D137. Pen and ink [1950]
11¹/₁₆ x 13⅞ (28.0 x 35.2)

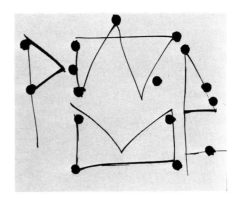

D140. Pen and ink, and brush and ink [1950]
11¹/₁₆ x 13⅞ (28.0 x 35.1)

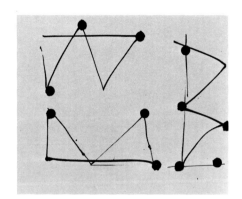

D141. Pen and ink, and brush
and ink   [1950]
11¹/₁₆ x 13⅞ (28.0 x 35.1)

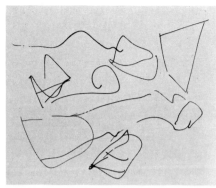

D144. Pen and ink   [1950]
11¹/₁₆ x 13⅞ (28.0 x 35.1)

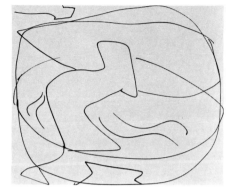

D147. Pen and ink   [1950]
11¹/₁₆ x 13⅞ (28.0 x 35.1)

D142. Pen and ink   [1950]
11¹/₁₆ x 13⅞ (28.0 x 35.1)

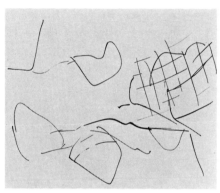

D145. Pen and ink   [1950]
11¹/₁₆ x 13⅞ (28.0 x 35.1)

D148. Pen and ink and colored
pencil   [1950]
11¹/₁₆ x 13¹³/₁₆ (28.0 x 35.1)

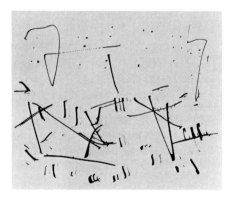

D143. Pen and ink   [1950]
11¹/₁₆ x 13⅞ (28.0 x 35.1)

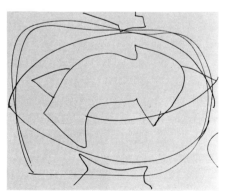

D146. Pen and ink   [1950]
11¹/₁₆ x 13⅞ (28.0 x 35.1)

D149. Pen and ink and colored
pencil   [1950]
11¹/₁₆ x 13¹³/₁₆ (28.0 x 35.1)

D150. Pen and ink and colored
pencil   [1950]
11¹/₁₆ x 13¹³/₁₆ (28.0 x 35.1)

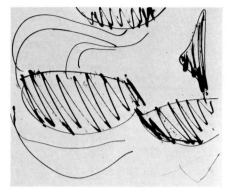

D153. Pen and ink and colored
pencil   [1950]
11¹/₁₆ x 13¹³/₁₆ (28.0 x 35.1)

D156. Pen and ink   [1948]
8⁵/₈ x 11¾ (21.9 x 29.7)

D151. Pen and ink   [1950]
11¹/₁₆ x 13¹³/₁₆ (28.0 x 35.1)

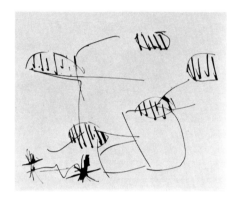

D154. Pen and ink   [1950]
11¹/₁₆ x 13¹³/₁₆ (28.0 x 35.1)

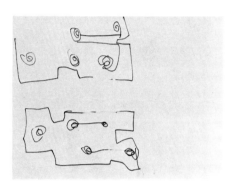

D157. Pen and ink   [1950]
9⁷/₈ x 13⁷/₈ (25.0 x 35.2)

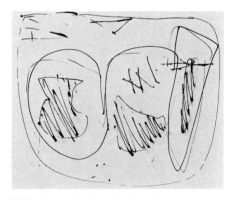

D152. Pen and ink and colored
pencil   [1950]
11¹/₁₆ x 13¹³/₁₆ (28.0 x 35.1)

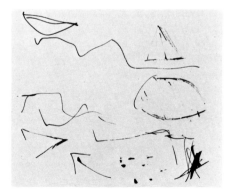

D155. Pen and ink   [1950]
11¹/₁₆ x 13¹³/₁₆ (28.0 x 35.1)

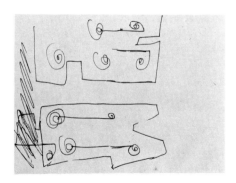

D158. Pen and ink   [1950]
9⁷/₈ x 13⁷/₈ (25.0 x 35.2)

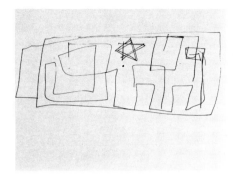

D159. Pen and ink   [1950]
9⅞ x 13⅞ (25.0 x 35.2)

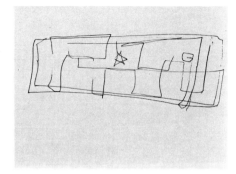

D162. Pen and ink   [1950]
9⅞ x 13⅞ (25.0 x 35.2)

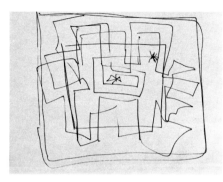

D165. Pen and ink   [1950]
9⅞ x 13⅞ (25.0 x 35.2)

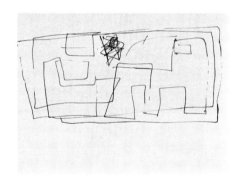

D160. Pen and ink   [1950]
9⅞ x 13⅞ (25.0 x 35.2)

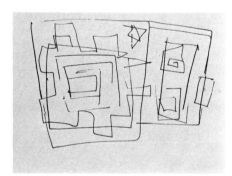

D163. Pen and ink   [1950]
9⅞ x 13⅞ (25.0 x 35.2)

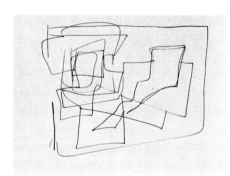

D166. Pen and ink   [1950]
9⅞ x 13⅞ (25.0 x 35.2)

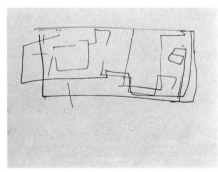

D161. Pen and ink   [1950]
9⅞ x 13⅞ (25.0 x 35.2)

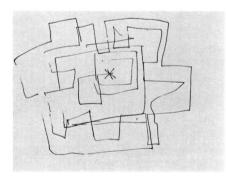

D164. Pen and ink   [1950]
9⅞ x 13⅞ (25.0 x 35.2)

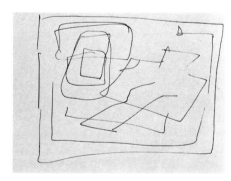

D167. Pen and ink   [1950]
9⅞ x 13⅞ (25.0 x 35.2)

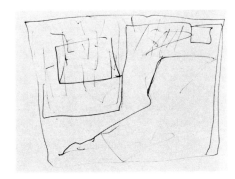

D168. Pen and ink   [1950]
9⅞ x 13⅞ (25.0 x 35.2)

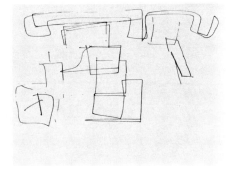

D171. Pen and ink   [1950]
9⅞ x 13⅞ (25.0 x 35.2)

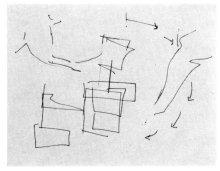

D174. Pen and ink   [1950]
9⅞ x 13⅞ (25.0 x 35.2)

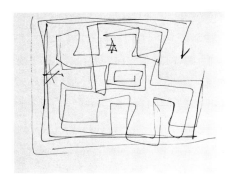

D169. Pen and ink   [1950]
9⅞ x 13⅞ (25.0 x 35.2)

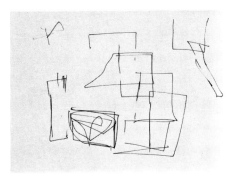

D172. Pen and ink   [1950]
9⅞ x 13⅞ (25.0 x 35.2)

D175. Pen and ink   [1950]
9⅞ x 13⅞ (25.0 x 35.2)

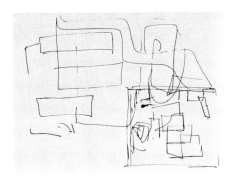

D170. Pen and ink   [1950]
9⅞ x 13⅞ (25.0 x 35.2)

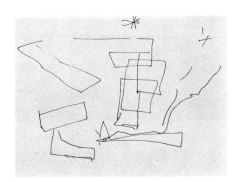

D173. Pen and ink   [1950]
9⅞ x 13⅞ (25.0 x 35.2)

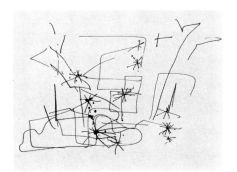

D176. Pen and ink   [1950]
9⅞ x 13⅞ (25.0 x 35.2)

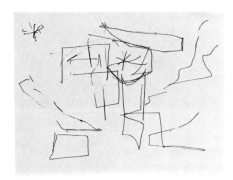

D177. Pen and ink   [1950]
9⅞ x 13⅞ (25.0 x 35.2)

D179. Pen and ink   [1950]
13⅞ x 11 (35.2 x 27.9)
Estate seal embossed lower left

D181. Pen and ink   [1950]
13⅞ x 11 (35.2 x 27.9)
Estate seal embossed upper right

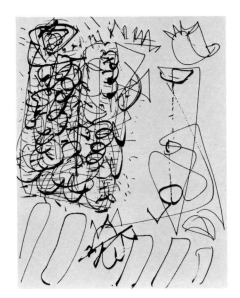

D178. Pen and ink   [1950]
13⅞ x 11 (35.1 x 27.9)
Estate seal embossed upper right

D180. Pen and ink   [1950]
13⅞ x 11 (35.2 x 27.9)
Estate seal embossed lower left

D182. Pen and ink   [1950]
13⅞ x 11 (35.2 x 27.9)
Estate seal embossed lower left

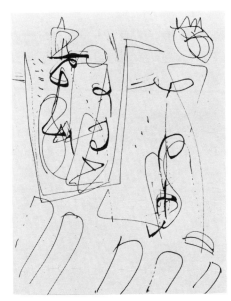

D183. Pen and ink   [1950]
13⅞ x 11 (35.2 x 27.9)
Estate seal embossed upper right

D185. Pen and ink   [1950]
11 x 13⅞ (27.9 x 35.2)

D187A. Pen and ink, pencil, and colored
pencil   [1950]
13¹³/₁₆ x 11 (35.0 x 27.8)

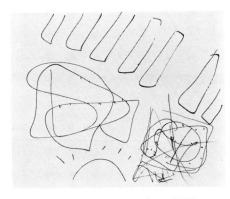

D184. Pen and ink and pencil   [1950]
11 x 13⅞ (27.9 x 35.2)

D186. Pen and ink   [1950]
11 x 13⅞ (27.9 x 35.2)

D187B. Pen and ink   [1950]
11 x 13¹³/₁₆ (27.8 x 35.0)
Estate seal embossed lower right in reverse

D188A. Pen and ink   [1950]
11 x 13¹³/₁₆ (27.8 x 35.1)

D189A. Pen and ink   [1950]
13¹³/₁₆ x 11 (35.1 x 27.8)
Estate seal embossed upper right

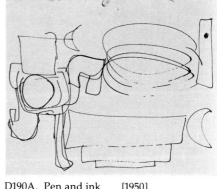

D190A. Pen and ink   [1950]
11 x 13¹³/₁₆ (27.8 x 35.1)

D188B. Pen and ink   [1950]
11 x 13¹³/₁₆ (27.8 x 35.1)
Estate seal embossed lower left in reverse

D189B. Pen and ink   [1950]
11 x 13¹³/₁₆ (27.8 x 35.1)
Estate seal embossed lower left in reverse

D190B. Pen and ink   [1950]
11 x 13¹³/₁₆ (27.8 x 35.1)
Estate seal embossed lower left in reverse

D191A. Pen and ink   [1950]
13¹³/₁₆ x 11 (35.1 x 27.8)
Estate seal embossed lower left

D192A. Pen and ink   [1950]
11 x 13¹³/₁₆ (27.9 x 35.1)

D193B. Pen and ink   [1950]
11 x 13⅞ (27.8 x 35.2)
Estate seal embossed lower left in reverse

D191B. Pen and ink   [1950]
11 x 13¹³/₁₆ (27.8 x 35.1)
Estate seal embossed lower left in reverse

D192B. Pen and ink   [1950]
11 x 13¹³/₁₆ (27.9 x 35.1)
Estate seal embossed lower left in reverse

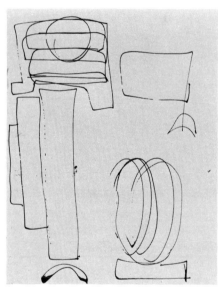

D194A. Pen and ink   [1950]
13¹³/₁₆ x 11 (35.1 x 27.8)

D193A. Pen and ink   [1950]
11 x 13⅞ (27.8 x 35.2)

D194B. Pen and ink   [1950]
11 x 13¹³/₁₆ (27.8 x 35.1)
Estate seal embossed upper left in reverse

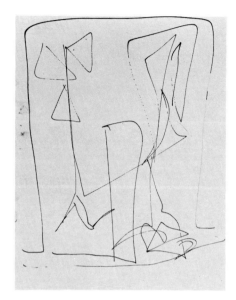

D195A. Pen and ink   [1950]
11 x 13¹³/₁₆ (27.8 x 35.1)

D196A. Pen and ink   [1950]
13⅞ x 11 (35.1 x 27.8)

D197A. Pen and ink and pencil   [1950]
13⅞ x 10⅞ (35.1 x 27.6)

D196B. Pen and ink   [1950]
11 x 13⅞ (27.8 x 35.1)
Estate seal embossed upper left in reverse

D197B. Pen and ink   [1950]
10⅞ x 13⅞ (27.6 x 35.1)
Estate seal embossed upper left in reverse

D195B. Pen and ink   [1950]
11 x 13¹³/₁₆ (27.8 x 35.1)
Estate seal embossed lower left in reverse

D198A. Pen and ink and pencil   [1950]
13¹³/₁₆ x 11 (35.1 x 27.8)

D199A. Pen and ink, pencil, and colored pencil   [1950]
13⅞ x 10⅞ (35.2 x 27.6)

D200A. Pen and ink and pencil   [1950]
13⅞ x 10⅞ (35.2 x 27.6)

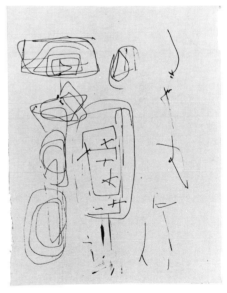

D198B. Pen and ink   [1950]
11 x 13¹³/₁₆ (27.8 x 35.1)
Estate seal embossed upper left in reverse

D199B. Pen and ink   [1950]
10⅞ x 13⅞ (27.6 x 35.2)
Estate seal embossed lower right in reverse

D200B. Pen and ink   [1950]
13⅞ x 10⅞ (35.2 x 27.6)
Estate seal embossed upper right in reverse

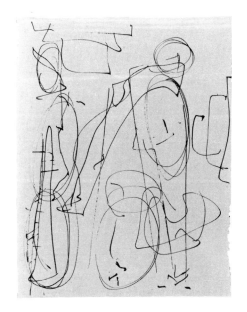

D203A. Pen and ink   [1950]
11 x 13¹³/₁₆ (27.8 x 35.1)

D201A. Pen and ink and pencil   [1950]
13⅞ x 10⅞ (35.1 x 27.6)

D202A. Pen and ink and pencil   [1950]
13⅞ x 10⅞ (35.2 x 27.6)

D203B. Pen and ink   [1950]
11 x 13¹³/₁₆ (27.8 x 35.1)
Estate seal embossed lower left in reverse

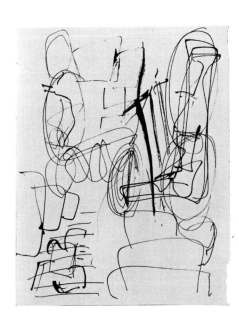

D201B. Pen and ink   [1950]
13⅞ x 10⅞ (35.1 x 27.6)
Estate seal embossed upper right in reverse

D202B. Pen and ink   [1950]
13⅞ x 10⅞ (35.2 x 27.6)
Estate seal embossed lower left in reverse

D204. Pen and ink   [1949]
18¾ x 23⅞ (47.6 x 60.5)

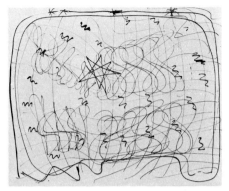

D205. Pen and ink   [1949–53]
18¾ x 23¹³/₁₆ (47.6 x 60.5)

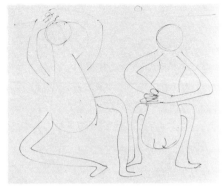

D208. Pen and ink   [1949]
18¾ x 23¹³/₁₆ (47.6 x 60.4)

D211. Pen and ink and pencil   [1949–53]
18¾ x 23¹³/₁₆ (47.6 x 60.4)

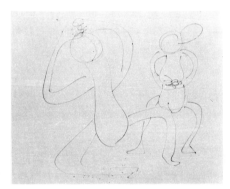

D206. Pen and ink   [1949]
18¾ x 23¹³/₁₆ (47.6 x 60.4)

D209. Pen and ink   [1949]
18¾ x 23¹³/₁₆ (47.6 x 60.4)

D212. Pen and ink, pencil, and colored
pencil   1953
18¾ x 23¹³/₁₆ (47.6 x 60.4)
Signed upper left in pencil: Louis 53

D207. Pen and ink   [1949]
18¾ x 23¹³/₁₆ (47.6 x 60.4)

D210. Pen and ink, pencil, and colored
pencil   [1953]
18¾ x 23¹³/₁₆ (47.6 x 60.4)

D213. Pen and ink   [1949]
18¾ x 23¹³/₁₆ (47.6 x 60.4)
No estate seal

D214. Pen and ink, pencil, and colored
pencil   1953
18¾ x 23¹³/₁₆ (47.6 x 60.4)
Signed lower left in pencil: Louis 53

D217. Pen and ink and pencil   1953
18¾ x 23⅞ (47.6 x 60.6)
Signed lower right in pencil: M. Louis 53

D220. Pen and ink and pencil   1953
18¾ x 23⅞ (47.6 x 60.6)
Signed lower right in pencil: Louis 53

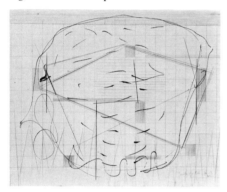

D215. *Geometry of a Fish*   1953
pen and ink, pencil, and colored pencil
18¾ x 23⅞ (47.6 x 60.5)
Signed lower right in pencil: Jan. 53 / Louis

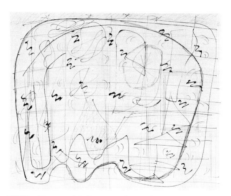

D218. Pen and ink, pencil, and colored
pencil   1953
18¾ x 23⅞ (47.5 x 60.5)
Signed lower center in pencil: Louis 53

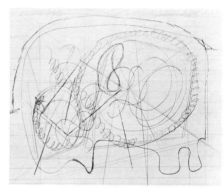

D221. Pencil and pen and ink   1953
18¾ x 23⅞ (47.6 x 60.6)
Signed upper left in pencil: Louis 53

D216. Pen and ink   [1953]
18¾ x 23⅞ (47.6 x 60.6)

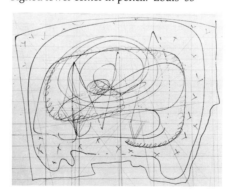

D219. Pen and ink and pencil   [1953]
18¾ x 23⅞ (47.5 x 60.5)

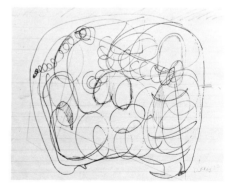

D222. Pen and ink and pencil   1953
18¾ x 23⅞ (47.6 x 60.5)
Signed lower right in pencil: Louis 53

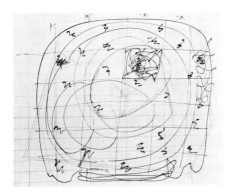

D223. Pen and ink and pencil   [1953]
18¾ x 23⅞ (47.5 x 60.5)

D226. Pencil, pen and ink, and colored
pencil   1953
18¹³/₁₆ x 23⅞ (47.7 x 60.5)
Signed upper right in pencil: Louis 53

D229. Pen and ink, brush and ink, and
colored pencil   [1953]
18¾ x 23⅞ (47.6 x 60.6)

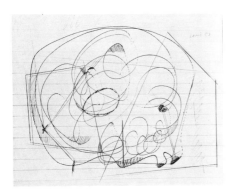

D224. Pencil and pen and ink   1953
18¾ x 23⅞ (47.6 x 60.6)
Signed upper right in pencil: Louis 53

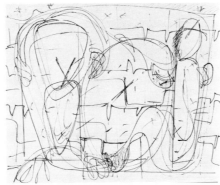

D227. Pen and ink, pencil, and colored
pencil   [1953]
18¾ x 23⅞ (47.6 x 60.5)

D230. Pencil, pen and ink, and colored
pencil   1953
18¾ x 23⅞ (47.6 x 60.5)
Signed upper right in pencil: Louis 53

D225. Pen and ink, pencil, and colored
pencil   [1953]
18¾ x 23⅞ (47.6 x 60.5)

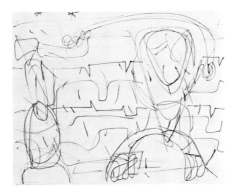

D228. Pen and ink and pencil   1953
18¾ x 23¹³/₁₆ (47.6 x 60.5)
Signed lower right in pencil: Louis 53

D231. Pen and ink and pencil   1953
18¾ x 23¹³/₁₆ (47.6 x 60.5)
Signed lower center in pencil: Louis 53
No estate seal

D232. Pen and ink   [1953]
18¾ x 23⅞ (47.6 x 60.5)

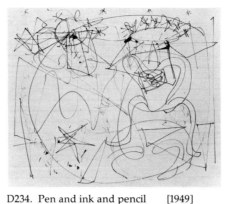

D234. Pen and ink and pencil   [1949]
18⅝ x 23⅝ (47.3 x 60.0)

D237. Pen and ink   [1949]
18⅝ x 23⅝ (47.2 x 60.0)

D233A. Pen and ink, and brush
and ink   [1949]
18⅝ x 23⅝ (47.2 x 60.0)

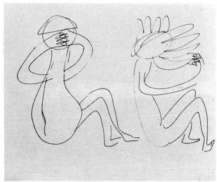

D235. Pen and ink   [1949]
18⅝ x 23⅝ (47.2 x 60.0)

D238. Pen and ink   [1949]
18⅝ x 23⅝ (47.3 x 60.0)

D233B. Pen and ink   [1949]
18⅝ x 23⅝ (47.2 x 60.0)
Estate seal embossed upper right in reverse

D236. Pen and ink   [1949]
18⅝ x 23⅝ (47.3 x 60.0)

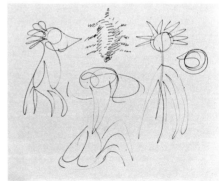

D239. Pen and ink   [1949]
18⅝ x 23⅝ (47.3 x 60.0)

D240. Pen and ink [1949]
18⅝ x 23⅝ (47.3 x 60.0)

D243. Pen and ink [1949]
18⅝ x 23⅝ (47.3 x 60.0)

D246. Pencil, pen and ink, and colored
pencil [1949–53]
18⅝ x 23⅝ (47.2 x 60.0)

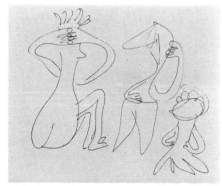

D241. Pen and ink [1949]
18⅝ x 23⅝ (47.2 x 60.0)

D244. Pen and ink [1949]
18⅝ x 23⅝ (47.3 x 60.0)

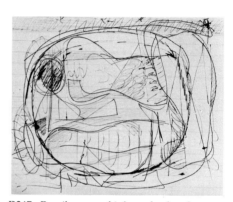

D247. Pencil, pen and ink, and colored
pencil [1949–53]
18⅝ x 23⅝ (47.2 x 60.0)

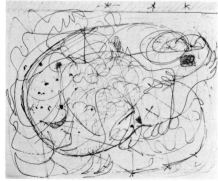

D242. Pen and ink, pencil, and colored
pencil 1953
18⅝ x 23⅝ (47.3 x 60.0)
Signed upper right in pencil: M Louis 53

D245. Pen and ink [1949]
18⅝ x 23⅝ (47.2 x 60.0)

D248. Pen and ink [1949]
18⅝ x 23⅝ (47.2 x 60.0)

D249. Pencil, pen and ink, and colored
pencil   1953
18¾ x 23¹¹/₁₆ (47.6 x 60.1)
Signed lower right in pencil: Louis 53

D252. Pen and ink, pencil, and colored
pencil   1953
18¾ x 23¹¹/₁₆ (47.6 x 60.1)
Signed lower right in pencil: Louis 53

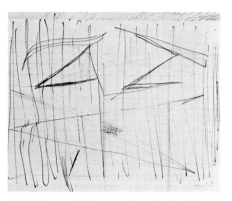

D255. Pen and ink, pencil, and colored
pencil   1953
18¾ x 23¹¹/₁₆ (47.6 x 60.1)
Signed lower right in pencil: Louis 53

D250. Pen and ink, pencil, and colored
pencil   1953
18¾ x 23¹¹/₁₆ (47.6 x 60.1)
Signed lower right in pencil: Louis 53

D253. Pen and ink, pencil, and colored
pencil   [1953]
18¾ x 23¹¹/₁₆ (47.6 x 60.1)

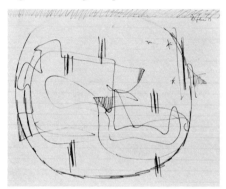

D256. Pen and ink and pencil   1953
18¾ x 23¹¹/₁₆ (47.6 x 60.1)
Signed upper right in pencil: M. Louis 53

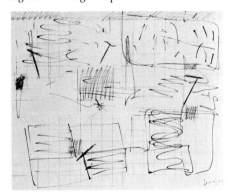

D251. Pen and ink, pencil, and colored
pencil   1953
18¾ x 23¹¹/₁₆ (47.6 x 60.1)
Signed lower right in pencil: Louis 53

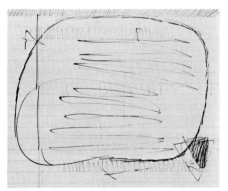

D254. Pen and ink, pencil, and colored
pencil   [1953]
18¾ x 23¹¹/₁₆ (47.6 x 60.1)

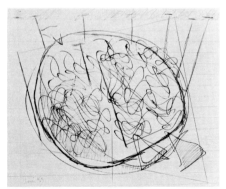

D257. Pen and ink and pencil   1953
18¾ x 23¹¹/₁₆ (47.6 x 60.1)
Signed lower left in pencil: Louis 53

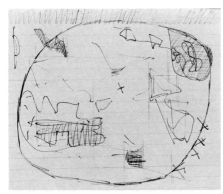

D258. Pen and ink, pencil, and colored
pencil   [1953]
18¾ x 23¹¹/₁₆ (47.6 x 60.1)

D261A. Pen and ink   [1953]
18¾ x 23¹³/₁₆ (47.6 x 60.4)

D263. Pen and ink, pencil, and colored
pencil   1953
18¾ x 23¹³/₁₆ (47.6 x 60.5)
Signed lower right in pencil: Louis 53

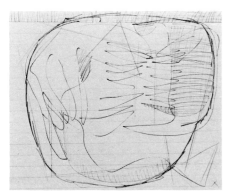

D259. Pen and ink, pencil, and colored
pencil   [1953]
18¾ x 23¹¹/₁₆ (47.6 x 60.1)

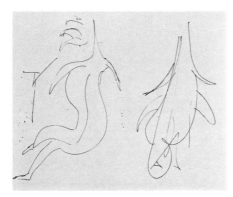

D261B. Pen and ink   [1953]
18¾ x 23¹³/₁₆ (47.6 x 60.4)
Estate seal embossed upper right in reverse

D264. Pen and ink and pencil   [1953]
18¾ x 23¹³/₁₆ (47.6 x 60.5)

D260. Pen and ink, pencil, and colored
pencil   1953
18¾ x 23¹¹/₁₆ (47.6 x 60.0)
Signed lower right in pencil: Louis 53

D262. Pen and ink, pencil, and colored
pencil   1953
18¾ x 23¹³/₁₆ (47.6 x 60.4)
Signed lower left in pencil: Louis 53

D265. Pen and ink   [1953]
18¾ x 23¹³/₁₆ (47.6 x 60.5)

D266. Pen and ink, pencil, and colored
pencil   [1953]
18¾ x 23¹³/₁₆ (47.6 x 60.5)

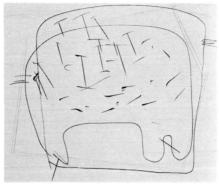

D269. Pen and ink and pencil   [1953]
18¾ x 23¹³/₁₆ (47.6 x 60.5)

D272. Pen and ink and pencil   [1953]
18¾ x 23¹³/₁₆ (47.6 x 60.5)

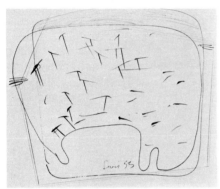

D267. Pen and ink and pencil   1953
18¾ x 23¹³/₁₆ (47.6 x 60.5)
Signed lower center in pencil: Louis 53

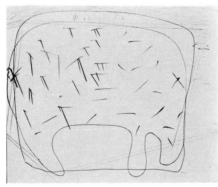

D270. Pencil and pen and ink   1953
18¾ x 23¹³/₁₆ (47.6 x 60.5)
Signed upper center in pencil: M. Louis 53

D273. Pen and ink and pencil   1953
18¾ x 23¹³/₁₆ (47.6 x 60.5)
Signed lower left in pencil: Louis 53

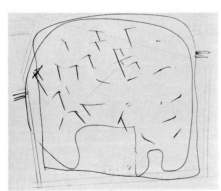

D268. Pen and ink and pencil   1953
18¾ x 23¹³/₁₆ (47.6 x 60.5)
Signed lower center in pencil: Louis 53

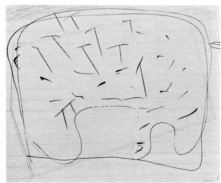

D271. Pen and ink and pencil   1953
18¾ x 23¹³/₁₆ (47.6 x 60.5)
Signed lower right in pencil: Louis 53

D274. Pen and ink and pencil   1953
18¾ x 23¹³/₁₆ (47.6 x 60.5)
Signed lower center in pencil: Louis 53

D275. Pen and ink and pencil   [1953]
18¾ x 23¹³/₁₆ (47.6 x 60.5)

D278. Pen and ink   [1953]
18¾ x 23¹³/₁₆ (47.5 x 60.5)

D281. Pen and ink, pencil, and colored
pencil   1953
18¹³/₁₆ x 23⅞ (47.6 x 60.6)
Signed upper left in pencil: Louis 53

D276. Pen and ink and pencil   [1953]
18¾ x 23¹³/₁₆ (47.6 x 60.5)

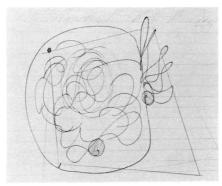

D279. Pen and ink and pencil   1953
18¾ x 23⅞ (47.6 x 60.6)
Signed upper right in pencil: Louis 53

D282. Pen and ink, pencil, and colored
pencil   1953
18¹³/₁₆ x 23¹⁵/₁₆ (47.7 x 60.7)
Signed upper center in pencil: Louis 53

D277. Pen and ink and pencil   [1953]
18¾ x 23¹³/₁₆ (47.6 x 60.5)

D280. Pen and ink, pencil, and colored
pencil   1953
18¹³/₁₆ x 23¹⁵/₁₆ (47.7 x 60.6)
Signed lower left in pencil: Louis 53

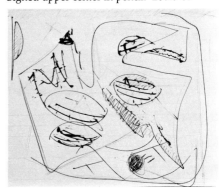

D283. Pen and ink, pencil, and colored
pencil   [1953]
18¹³/₁₆ x 23¹⁵/₁₆ (47.7 x 60.7)

D284. Pen and ink, pencil, and colored
pencil   [1953]
18¹³/₁₆ x 23⅞ (47.7 x 60.7)

D287. Pen and ink, and brush
and ink   [1953]
18¹³/₁₆ x 23⅞ (47.7 x 60.7)

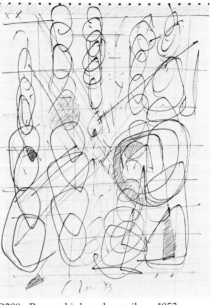

D289. Pen and ink and pencil   1953
19¹³/₁₆ x 14⅞ (50.3 x 37.7)
Signed lower center in pencil: Louis 53

D285. Pen and ink, pencil, and colored
pencil   [1953]
18¹³/₁₆ x 23⅞ (47.7 x 60.6)

D288. Pen and ink, pencil, and colored
pencil   [1953]
18¹³/₁₆ x 23¹⁵/₁₆ (47.7 x 60.7)

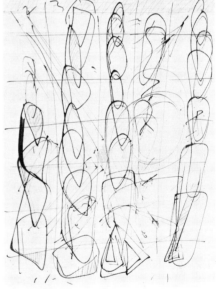

D290. Pen and ink and pencil   1953
19¹³/₁₆ x 14⅞ (50.3 x 37.7)
Signed lower right in pencil: Louis 53

D286. Pen and ink, pencil, and colored
pencil   [1953]
18¹³/₁₆ x 23⅞ (47.7 x 60.7)

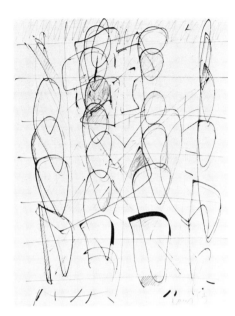

D291. Pencil and pen and ink   1953
19¹³/₁₆ x 14¹³/₁₆ (50.3 x 37.6)
Signed lower right in pencil: Louis 53

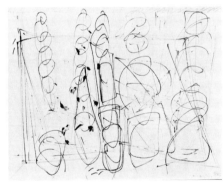

D292. Pen and ink and pencil   1953
14⅞ x 19¹³/₁₆ (37.7 x 50.3)
Signed lower right in pencil: Louis 53

D293. Pen and ink and pencil   [1953]
14⅞ x 19¹³/₁₆ (37.7 x 50.3)

D294. Pen and ink and pencil   [1953]
14⅞ x 19¹³/₁₆ (37.7 x 50.3)

D295. Pen and ink, pencil, and colored
pencil   [1953]
14⅞ x 19¹³/₁₆ (37.7 x 50.3)

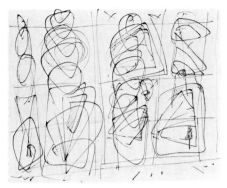

D296. Pen and ink and pencil   1953
14⅞ x 19¹³/₁₆ (37.7 x 50.3)
Signed upper left in pencil: Louis 53

D297. Pen and ink and pencil   [1953]
14⅞ x 19¹³/₁₆ (37.7 x 50.3)

D298. Pen and ink and pencil   1953
14⅞ x 19¹³/₁₆ (37.7 x 50.3)
Signed upper center in pencil: Louis 53

D299. Pen and ink and pencil [1953]
14⅞ x 19¹³/₁₆ (37.7 x 50.3)

D302. Pen and ink and pencil 1953
14⅞ x 19¹³/₁₆ (37.6 x 50.3)
Signed lower right in pencil: Louis 53

D305. Pen and ink and pencil 1953
14⅞ x 19¹³/₁₆ (37.7 x 50.3)
Signed lower right in pencil: Louis 53

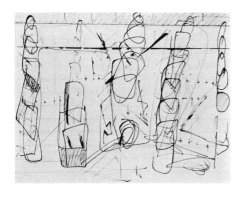

D300. Pen and ink, pencil, and colored
pencil [1953]
14⅞ x 19¹³/₁₆ (37.7 x 50.3)

D303. Pen and ink, pencil, and colored
pencil [1953]
14⅞ x 19¹³/₁₆ (37.7 x 50.3)

D306. Pen and ink and pencil 1953
14⅞ x 19¹³/₁₆ (37.7 x 50.3)
Signed lower right in pencil: Louis 53

D301. Pen and ink and pencil 1953
14⅞ x 19¹³/₁₆ (37.7 x 50.3)
Signed upper right in pencil: Louis 53;
and lower right in pencil erased: Louis 53

D304. Pen and ink and pencil [1953]
14⅞ x 19¹³/₁₆ (37.7 x 50.3)

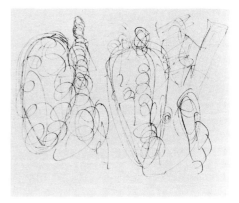

D307. Pen and ink [1950–53]
13¹³/₁₆ x 16¹⁵/₁₆ (35.0 x 42.9)

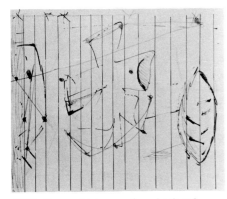

D308. Pen and ink, pencil, and colored
pencil   [1950–53]
13¹³/₁₆ x 16¹⁵/₁₆ (35.0 x 42.9)

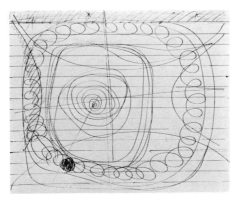

D311. Pen and ink, pencil, and colored
pencil   [1950–53]
13¹³/₁₆ x 16¹⁵/₁₆ (35.0 x 42.9)

D314. Pen and ink, pencil, and colored
pencil   [1950–53]
13¹³/₁₆ x 16¹⁵/₁₆ (35.0 x 42.9)

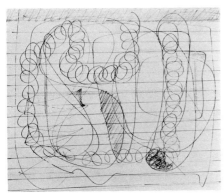

D309. Pen and ink, pencil, and colored
pencil   [1950–53]
13¹³/₁₆ x 16¹⁵/₁₆ (35.0 x 42.9)

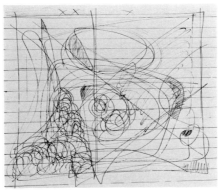

D312. Pen and ink and pencil   [1950–53]
13¹³/₁₆ x 16¹⁵/₁₆ (35.0 x 42.9)

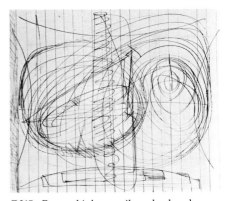

D315. Pen and ink, pencil, and colored
pencil   [1950–53]
13¹³/₁₆ x 16¹⁵/₁₆ (35.0 x 42.9)

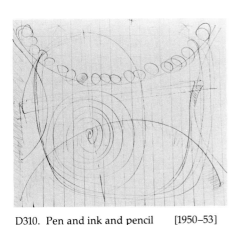

D310. Pen and ink and pencil   [1950–53]
13¹³/₁₆ x 16¹⁵/₁₆ (35.0 x 42.9)

D313. Pen and ink, pencil, and colored
pencil   [1950–53]
13¹³/₁₆ x 16¹⁵/₁₆ (35.0 x 42.9)

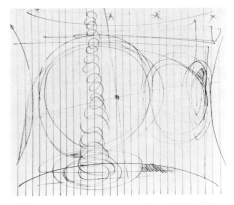

D316. Pen and ink and pencil   [1950–53]
13¹³/₁₆ x 16¹⁵/₁₆ (35.0 x 42.9)

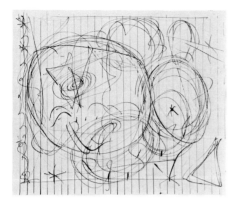

D317. Pen and ink and colored
pencil   [1950–53]
13¹³/₁₆ x 16⅞ (35.0 x 42.9)

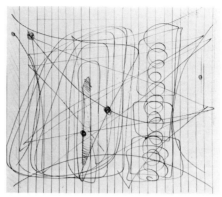

D320. Pen and ink and pencil   [1950–53]
13¹³/₁₆ x 16¹⁵/₁₆ (35.0 x 42.9)

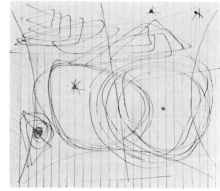

D323. Pen and ink and pencil   [1950–53]
13¹³/₁₆ x 16¹⁵/₁₆ (35.0 x 42.9)

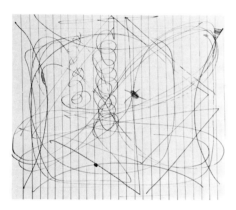

D318. Pen and ink and pencil   [1950–53]
13¹³/₁₆ x 16¹⁵/₁₆ (35.0 x 42.9)

D321. Pen and ink and pencil   [1950–53]
13¹³/₁₆ x 16¹⁵/₁₆ (35.0 x 42.9)

D324. Pen and ink and colored
pencil   [1950–53]
13¹³/₁₆ x 16¹⁵/₁₆ (35.0 x 42.9)

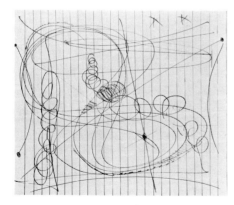

D319. Pen and ink and pencil   [1950–53]
13¹³/₁₆ x 16¹⁵/₁₆ (35.0 x 42.9)

D322. Pen and ink and colored
pencil   [1950–53]
13¹³/₁₆ x 16¹⁵/₁₆ (35.0 x 42.9)

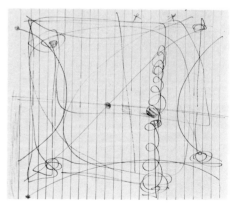

D325. Pen and ink and pencil   [1950–53]
13¹³/₁₆ x 16¹⁵/₁₆ (35.0 x 42.9)

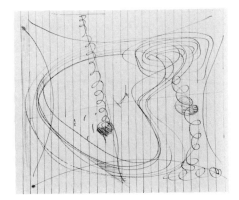

D326. Pen and ink and pencil   [1950–53]
13¹³/₁₆ x 16¹⁵/₁₆ (35.0 x 42.9)

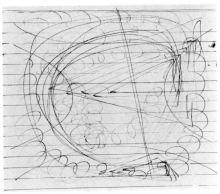

D329. Pen and ink   [1950–53]
13¹³/₁₆ x 16¹⁵/₁₆ (35.0 x 42.9)

D332. Pen and ink, brush and ink, and
colored pencil   [1950–53]
13¹³/₁₆ x 16¹⁵/₁₆ (35.0 x 42.9)

D327. Pen and ink and pencil   [1950–53]
13¹³/₁₆ x 16¹⁵/₁₆ (35.0 x 42.9)

D330. Pen and ink and pencil   [1950–53]
13¹³/₁₆ x 16¹⁵/₁₆ (35.0 x 42.9)

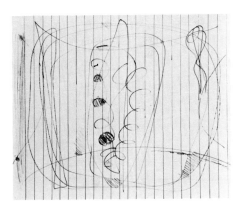

D333. Pen and ink and pencil   [1950–53]
13¹³/₁₆ x 16¹⁵/₁₆ (35.0 x 42.9)

D328. Pen and ink and colored
pencil   [1950–53]
13¹³/₁₆ x 16¹⁵/₁₆ (35.0 x 42.9)

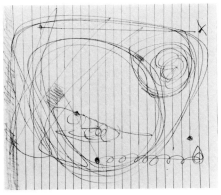

D331. Pen and ink and pencil   [1950–53]
13¹³/₁₆ x 16¹⁵/₁₆ (35.0 x 42.9)

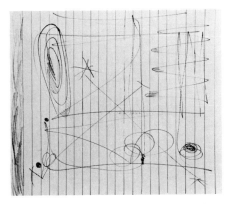

D334. Pen and ink and pencil   [1950–53]
13¹³/₁₆ x 16¹⁵/₁₆ (35.0 x 42.9)

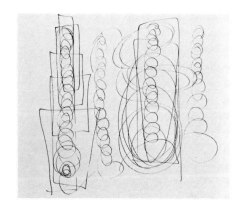

D335. Pen and ink   [1950–53]
13¹³/₁₆ x 16¹⁵/₁₆ (35.0 x 42.9)

D338. Pen and ink   [1950–53]
13¹³/₁₆ x 16¹⁵/₁₆ (35.0 x 42.9)

D341. Pen and ink and colored
pencil   [1950–53]
13¹³/₁₆ x 16¹⁵/₁₆ (35.0 x 42.9)

D336. Pen and ink, brush and ink, and
colored pencil   [1950–53]
13¹³/₁₆ x 16¹⁵/₁₆ (35.0 x 42.9)

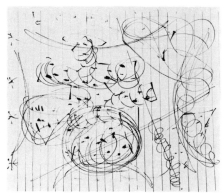

D339. Pen and ink and colored
pencil   [1950–53]
13¹³/₁₆ x 16¹⁵/₁₆ (35.0 x 42.9)

D342. Pen and ink, pencil, and colored
pencil   [1950–53]
irregular: 13¹³/₁₆ x 16¹⁵/₁₆ (35.0 x 42.9)

D337. Pen and ink, brush and ink, and
colored pencil   [1950–53]
13¹³/₁₆ x 16¹⁵/₁₆ (35.0 x 42.9)

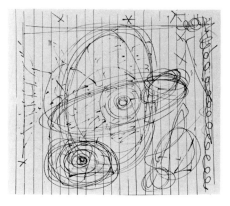

D340. Pen and ink and colored
pencil   [1950–53]
13¹³/₁₆ x 16¹⁵/₁₆ (35.0 x 42.9)

D343. Pen and ink and colored
pencil   [1950–53]
irregular: 13¹³/₁₆ x 16¹⁵/₁₆ (35.0 x 42.9)

118

D344. Pen and ink and colored
pencil   [1950–53]
13¹³/₁₆ x 16¹⁵/₁₆ (35.0 x 42.9)

D347. Pen and ink and pencil   [1950–53]
14¹/₁₆ x 16¹⁵/₁₆ (35.6 x 42.9)

D350. Pen and ink   [1950–53]
14¹/₁₆ x 16¹⁵/₁₆ (35.7 x 42.9)

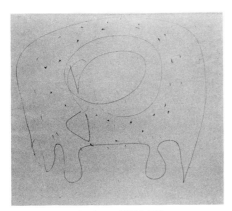

D345. Pen and ink   [1950–53]
14¹/₁₆ x 16¹⁵/₁₆ (35.6 x 43.0)

D348. Pen and ink   [1950–53]
14¹/₁₆ x 16¹⁵/₁₆ (35.6 x 42.9)

D351. Pen and ink   [1950–53]
14¹/₁₆ x 16¹⁵/₁₆ (35.6 x 42.9)

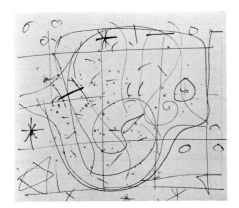

D346. Pen and ink, colored ink, and
pencil   [1950–53]
14¹/₁₆ x 16¹⁵/₁₆ (35.6 x 42.9)

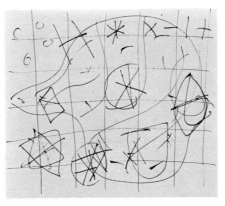

D349. Pen and ink and pencil   [1950–53]
14¹/₁₆ x 16¹⁵/₁₆ (35.7 x 42.9)

D352. Pen and ink and pencil   [1950–53]
14¹/₁₆ x 16¹⁵/₁₆ (35.6 x 42.9)

D353. Pen and ink   [1950–53]
14¹/₁₆ x 16¹⁵/₁₆ (35.6 x 42.9)

D356. Pen and ink, pencil, and colored pencil   [1950–53]
14¹/₁₆ x 16¹⁵/₁₆ (35.7 x 42.9)

D359. Pen and ink   [1950–53]
14¹/₁₆ x 16¹⁵/₁₆ (35.6 x 42.9)

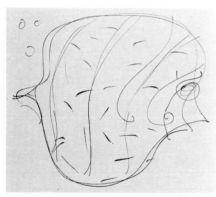

D354. Pen and ink   [1950–53]
14¹/₁₆ x 16¹⁵/₁₆ (35.7 x 42.9)

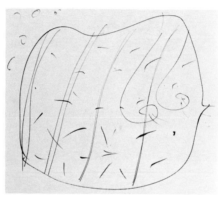

D357. Pen and ink   [1950–53]
14¹/₁₆ x 16¹⁵/₁₆ (35.6 x 42.9)

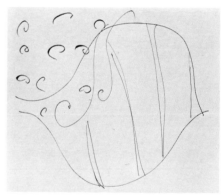

D360. Pen and ink   [1950–53]
14¹/₁₆ x 16¹⁵/₁₆ (35.6 x 42.9)

D355. Pen and ink   [1950–53]
14¹/₁₆ x 16¹⁵/₁₆ (35.7 x 42.9)

D358. Pen and ink   [1950–53]
14¹/₁₆ x 16¹⁵/₁₆ (35.6 x 42.9)

D361. Pen and ink and pencil   [1950–53]
14¹/₁₆ x 16¹⁵/₁₆ (35.6 x 42.9)

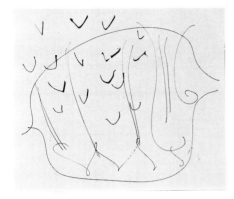

D362. Pen and ink   [1950–53]
14 1/16 x 16 15/16 (35.6 x 42.9)

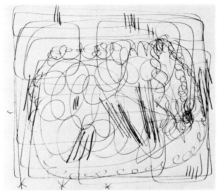

D365A. Pen and ink   [1950–53]
14 1/16 x 16 15/16 (35.6 x 42.9)

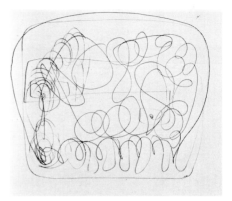

D367. Pen and ink   [1950–53]
14 1/16 x 16 15/16 (35.6 x 42.9)

D363. Pen and ink and pencil   [1950–53]
14 1/16 x 16 15/16 (35.6 x 42.9)

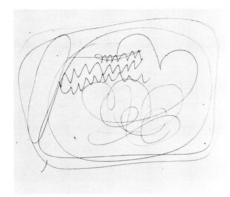

D365B. Pen and ink   [1950–53]
14 1/16 x 16 15/16 (35.6 x 42.9)
Estate seal embossed lower left in reverse

D368. Pen and ink   [1950–53]
14 1/16 x 16 15/16 (35.6 x 43.0)

D364. Pen and ink   [1950–53]
14 1/16 x 16 15/16 (35.6 x 42.9)

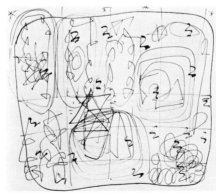

D366. Pen and ink   [1950–53]
14 1/16 x 16 15/16 (35.6 x 42.9)

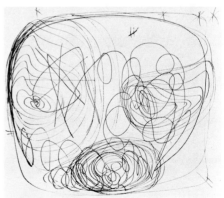

D369. Pen and ink   [1950–53]
14 1/16 x 16 15/16 (35.6 x 43.0)

D370. Pen and ink   [1950–53]
14 1/16 x 16 15/16 (35.6 x 43.0)

D373. Pen and ink   [1950–53]
14 1/16 x 16 15/16 (35.6 x 43.0)

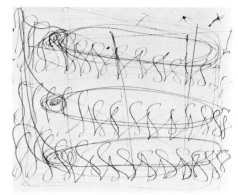

D376. Pen and ink and pencil   [1950–53]
14 1/16 x 16 15/16 (35.6 x 43.0)

D371. Pen and ink   [1950–53]
14 1/16 x 16 15/16 (35.6 x 43.0)

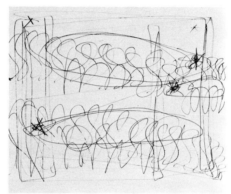

D374. Pen and ink   [1950–53]
14 1/16 x 16 15/16 (35.6 x 42.9)

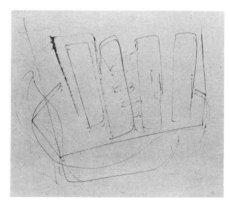

D377. Pen and ink   [1950–53]
13 15/16 x 16 13/16 (35.3 x 42.7)

D372. Pen and ink   [1950–53]
14 1/16 x 16 15/16 (35.6 x 43.0)

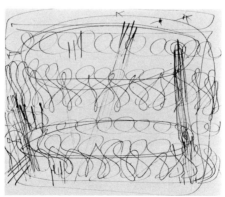

D375. Pen and ink   [1950–53]
14 1/16 x 16 15/16 (35.6 x 42.9)

D378. Pen and ink, pencil, and colored
pencil   [1950–53]
13 7/8 x 16 13/16 (35.3 x 42.6)

D379. Pen and ink, pencil, and colored
pencil   [1950–53]
13⅞ x 16¹³/₁₆ (35.3 x 42.6)

D381B. Pen and ink, and brush and
ink   [1950–53]
13¹⁵/₁₆ x 16¹³/₁₆ (35.3 x 42.6)
Estate seal embossed lower left in reverse

D384. Pen and ink, pencil, and colored
pencil   [1950–53]
13¹⁵/₁₆ x 16¹³/₁₆ (35.3 x 42.6)

D380. Pen and ink, pencil, and colored
pencil   [1950–53]
13¹⁵/₁₆ x 16¹³/₁₆ (35.3 x 42.6)

D382. Pen and ink, pencil, and colored
pencil   [1950–53]
13¹⁵/₁₆ x 16¹³/₁₆ (35.3 x 42.6)

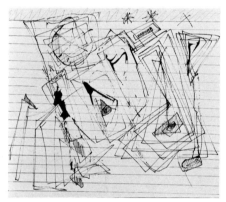

D385A. Pen and ink, pencil, and colored
pencil   [1950–53]
13¹⁵/₁₆ x 16¹³/₁₆ (35.3 x 42.6)

D381A. Pen and ink, pencil, and colored
pencil   [1950–53]
13¹⁵/₁₆ x 16¹³/₁₆ (35.3 x 42.6)

D383. Pen and ink, pencil, and colored
pencil   [1950–53]
13¹⁵/₁₆ x 16¹³/₁₆ (35.3 x 42.6)

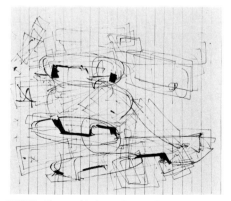

D385B. Pen and ink   [1950–53]
13¹⁵/₁₆ x 16¹³/₁₆ (35.3 x 42.6)
Estate seal embossed lower left in reverse

D386A. Pen and ink, pencil, and colored
pencil   [1950–53]
13¹⁵/₁₆ x 16¹³/₁₆ (35.3 x 42.6)

D388. Pen and ink, pencil, and colored
pencil   [1950–53]
13¹⁵/₁₆ x 16¹³/₁₆ (35.3 x 42.6)

D390B. Pen and ink   [1950–53]
13¹⁵/₁₆ x 16¹³/₁₆ (35.3 x 42.6)
Estate seal embossed lower left in reverse

D386B. Pen and ink   [1950–53]
13¹⁵/₁₆ x 16¹³/₁₆ (35.3 x 42.6)
Estate seal embossed lower left in reverse

D389. Pen and ink, pencil, and colored
pencil   [1950–53]
13¹⁵/₁₆ x 16¹³/₁₆ (35.3 x 42.6)

D391. Pen and ink, pencil, and colored
pencil   [1950–53]
13¹⁵/₁₆ x 16¹³/₁₆ (35.3 x 42.6)

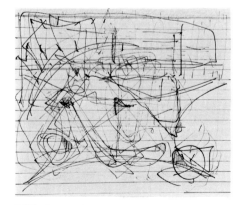

D387. Pen and ink, pencil, and colored
pencil   [1950–53]
13¹⁵/₁₆ x 16¹³/₁₆ (35.3 x 42.6)

D390A. Pen and ink, pencil, and colored
pencil   [1950–53]
13¹⁵/₁₆ x 16¹³/₁₆ (35.3 x 42.6)

D392A. Pen and ink, pencil, and colored
pencil   [1950–53]
13¹⁵/₁₆ x 16¹³/₁₆ (35.3 x 42.6)

D392B. Pen and ink   [1950–53]
13¹⁵/₁₆ x 16¹³/₁₆ (35.3 x 42.6)
Estate seal embossed lower left in reverse

D394A. Pen and ink, pencil, and colored
pencil   [1950–53]
13¹⁵/₁₆ x 16¹³/₁₆ (35.3 x 42.6)

D395B. Pen and ink   [1950–53]
13¹⁵/₁₆ x 16¹³/₁₆ (35.3 x 42.6)
Estate seal embossed lower left in reverse

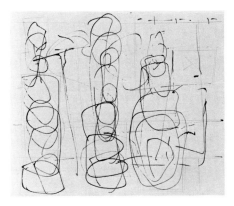

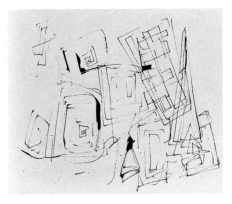

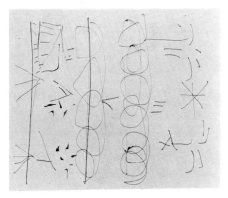

D393A. Pen and ink and pencil   [1950–53]
13¹⁵/₁₆ x 16¹³/₁₆ (35.3 x 42.6)

D394B. Pen and ink   [1950–53]
13¹⁵/₁₆ x 16¹³/₁₆ (35.3 x 42.6)
Estate seal embossed lower left in reverse

D396. Pen and ink   [1950–53]
11¹/₁₆ x 13⁷/₈ (28.0 x 35.2)

D393B. Pen and ink, and brush and
ink   [1950–53]
13¹⁵/₁₆ x 16¹³/₁₆ (35.3 x 42.6)
Estate seal embossed lower left in reverse

D395A. Pen and ink, pencil, and colored
pencil   [1950–53]
13¹⁵/₁₆ x 16¹³/₁₆ (35.3 x 42.6)

D397. Pen and ink   [1953]
13⁷/₈ x 16¹³/₁₆ (35.3 x 42.6)

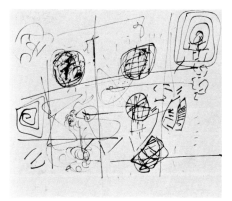

D398. Pen and ink, pencil, and colored ink   1953
13⅞ x 16¾ (35.2 x 42.5)
Signed upper left in pencil: Louis 53

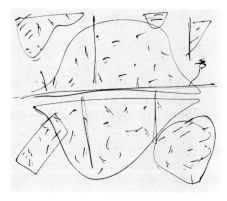

D401. Pen and ink   [1953]
13⅞ x 16¹³/₁₆ (35.2 x 42.6)

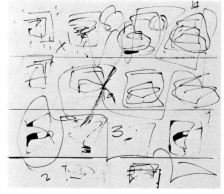

D404. Pen and ink   [1953]
13⅞ x 16¹³/₁₆ (35.2 x 42.6)

D399. Pen and ink, pencil, and colored pencil   1953
13⅞ x 16¾ (35.2 x 42.5)
Signed lower right in pencil: Louis 53

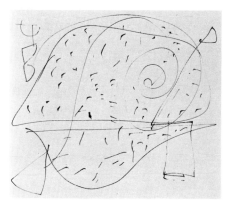

D402. Pen and ink   [1953]
13⅞ x 16¹³/₁₆ (35.2 x 42.6)

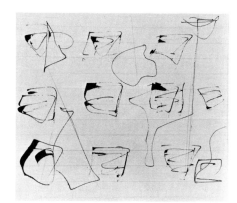

D405. Pen and ink and pencil   [1953]
13⅞ x 16¹³/₁₆ (35.2 x 42.6)

D400. Pen and ink, pencil, and colored pencil   [1953]
13⅞ x 16¹³/₁₆ (35.2 x 42.6)

D403. Pen and ink, pencil, and colored pencil   1953
13⅞ x 16¹³/₁₆ (35.2 x 42.6)
Signed upper left in pencil: Louis 53

D406. Pen and ink   [1953]
13⅞ x 16¹³/₁₆ (35.2 x 42.6)

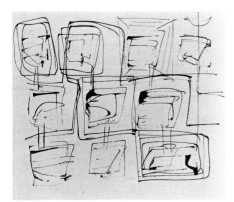

D407. Pen and ink   [1953]
13⅞ x 16¹³/₁₆ (35.2 x 42.6)

D410. Pen and ink   [1953]
13⅞ x 16¹³/₁₆ (35.2 x 42.6)

D413. Pen and ink   [1950–53]
14 x 16¹⁵/₁₆ (35.5 x 42.9)

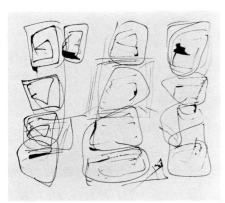

D408. Pen and ink   [1953]
13⅞ x 16¹³/₁₆ (35.2 x 42.6)

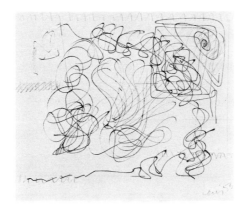

D411. Pen and ink, pencil, and colored
pencil   1953
13⅞ x 16¹³/₁₆ (35.2 x 42.6)
Signed lower right in pencil: Louis 53

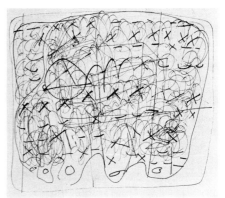

D414. Pen and ink   [1950–53]
14 x 16¹⁵/₁₆ (35.5 x 42.9)

D409. Pen and ink   [1953]
13⅞ x 16¹³/₁₆ (35.2 x 42.6)

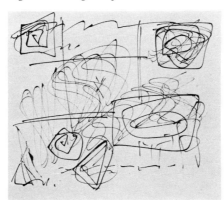

D412. Pen and ink   [1953]
13⅞ x 16¹³/₁₆ (35.2 x 42.6)

D415. Pen and ink   [1950–53]
14 x 16¹⁵/₁₆ (35.5 x 42.9)

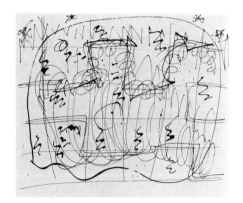

D416. Pen and ink   [1950–53]
14 x 16¹⁵/₁₆ (35.5 x 42.9)

D419. Pen and ink   [1950–53]
14 x 16¹⁵/₁₆ (35.5 x 42.9)

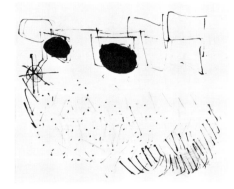

D422. Pen and ink and colored
pencil   [1950–53]
11 x 14 (27.9 x 35.4)

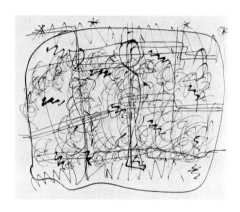

D417. Pen and ink   [1950–53]
14 x 16¹⁵/₁₆ (35.5 x 42.9)

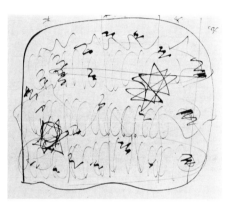

D420. Pen and ink   [1950–53]
14 x 16¹⁵/₁₆ (35.5 x 42.9)

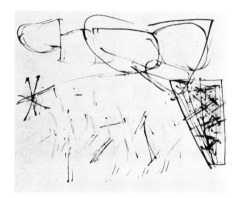

D423. Pen and ink and colored
pencil   [1950–53]
11 x 14 (27.9 x 35.5)

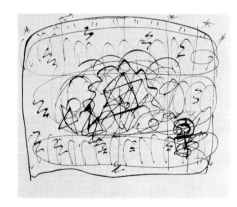

D418. Pen and ink and pencil   [1950–53]
14 x 16¹⁵/₁₆ (35.5 x 42.9)

D421. Pen and ink and colored
pencil   [1950–53]
11 x 14 (27.9 x 35.4)

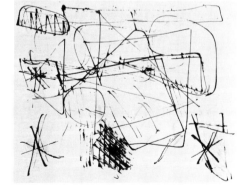

D424. Pen and ink and colored
pencil   [1950–53]
11 x 14 (27.9 x 35.5)

D425. Pen and ink and colored
pencil   [1950–53]
11 x 14 (27.9 x 35.4)

D427B. Pen and ink, and brush and
ink   [1950–53]
11 x 14 (27.8 x 35.5)
Estate seal embossed lower left in reverse

D430. Pen and ink   [1950–53]
13⅞ x 16¹³/₁₆ (35.2 x 42.6)

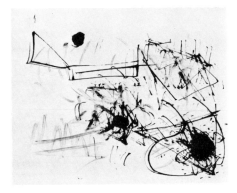

D426. Pen and ink and colored
pencil   [1950–53]
11 x 14 (27.8 x 35.5)

D428. Pencil   [1950–53]
13⅞ x 16¹³/₁₆ (35.2 x 42.6)

D431. Pen and ink   [1950–53]
13⅞ x 16¹³/₁₆ (35.2 x 42.6)

D427A. Pen and ink and colored
pencil   [1950–53]
11 x 14 (27.8 x 35.5)

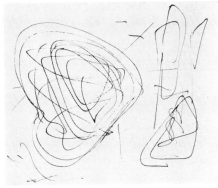

D429. Pen and ink *   [1950–53]
13⅞ x 16¹³/₁₆ (35.2 x 42.6)

D432. Pen and ink   [1950–53]
13⅞ x 16¹³/₁₆ (35.2 x 42.6)

129

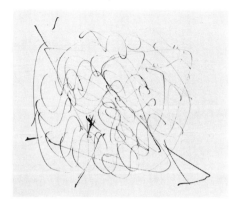

D433. Pen and ink   [1950–53]
13⅞ x 16¹³/₁₆ (35.2 x 42.6)

D436. Pen and ink, pencil, and colored
pencil   1953
13⅞ x 16¹³/₁₆ (35.2 x 42.6)
Signed lower right in pencil: Louis 53

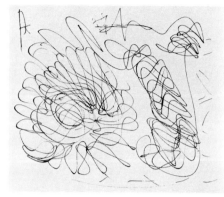

D439. Pen and ink   [1950–53]
13⅞ x 16¹³/₁₆ (35.2 x 42.6)

D434. Pen and ink   [1950–53]
13⅞ x 16¹³/₁₆ (35.2 x 42.6)

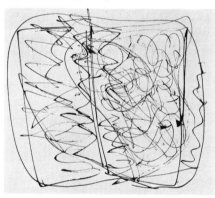

D437. Pen and ink   [1950–53]
13⅞ x 16¹³/₁₆ (35.2 x 42.6)

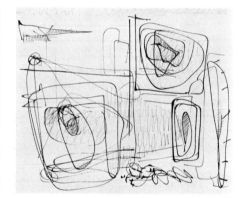

D440. Pen and ink, pencil, and colored
pencil   [1950–53]
13⅞ x 16¹³/₁₆ (35.2 x 42.6)

D435. Pen and ink   [1950–53]
13⅞ x 16¹³/₁₆ (35.2 x 42.6)

D438. Pen and ink   [1950–53]
13⅞ x 16¹³/₁₆ (35.2 x 42.6)

D441. Pen and ink, pencil, and colored
pencil   [1950–53]
13⅞ x 16¹³/₁₆ (35.2 x 42.6)

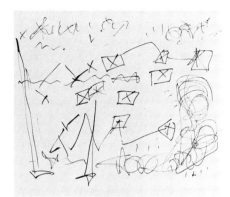

D442. Pen and ink, pencil, and colored
pencil   [1950–53]
13⅞ x 16¹³/₁₆ (35.2 x 42.6)

D445. Pen and ink   [1950–53]
13⅞ x 16¹³/₁₆ (35.2 x 42.6)

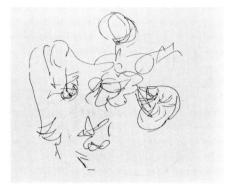

D447B. Pen and ink and colored
pencil   [1950–53]
11 x 13¹⁵/₁₆ (27.9 x 35.3)
Estate seal embossed lower left in reverse

D443. Pen and ink, pencil, and colored
pencil   [1950–53]
13⅞ x 16¹³/₁₆ (35.2 x 42.6)

D446. Pen and ink   [1950–53]
10¹⁵/₁₆ x 13¹⁵/₁₆ (27.8 x 35.4)

D448. Pen and ink   [1950–53]
8⅞ x 11¹⁵/₁₆ (22.5 x 30.3)

D444. Pen and ink, pencil, and colored
pencil   [1950–53]
13⅞ x 16¹³/₁₆ (35.2 x 42.6)

D447A. Pen and ink and colored
pencil   [1950–53]
11 x 13¹⁵/₁₆ (27.9 x 35.3)

D449A. Pen and ink   [1950–53]
8¹¹/₁₆ x 11¹¹/₁₆ (22.0 x 29.7)

131

D449B. Pen and ink   [1950–53]
8¹¹/₁₆ x 11¹¹/₁₆ (22.0 x 29.7)
Estate seal embossed lower left in reverse

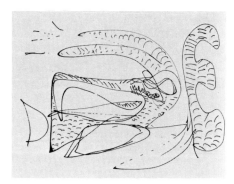

D451. Pen and ink   [1950–53]
8⅞ x 11¹⁵/₁₆ (22.5 x 30.3)

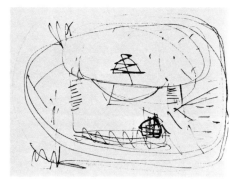

D454A. Pen and ink and colored
pencil   [1950–53]
8⅞ x 11⅞ (22.5 x 30.1)

D450A. Pen and ink   [1950–53]
8¹¹/₁₆ x 11¹¹/₁₆ (22.1 x 29.6)

D452. Pen and ink   [1950–53]
8⅞ x 11¹⁵/₁₆ (22.5 x 30.3)

D454B. Pen and ink   [1950–53]
8⅞ x 11⅞ (22.5 x 30.1)
Estate seal embossed lower left in reverse

D450B. Pen and ink   [1950–53]
8¹¹/₁₆ x 11¹¹/₁₆ (22.1 x 29.6)
Estate seal embossed lower left in reverse

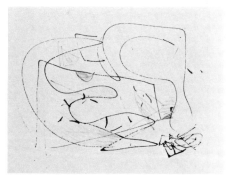

D453. Pen and ink   [1950–53]
8⅞ x 11¹⁵/₁₆ (22.5 x 30.3)

D455A. Pen and ink, pencil, and colored
pencil   [1950–53]
8⅞ x 11⅞ (22.5 x 30.1)

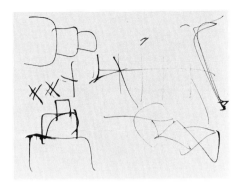

D455B. Pen and ink   [1950–53]
8⅞ x 11⅞ (22.5 x 30.1)
Estate seal embossed lower left in reverse

D457A. Pen and ink, pencil, and colored
pencil   [1950–53]
8⅞ x 11⅞ (22.5 x 30.1)

D458B. Pen and ink   [1950–53]
8⅞ x 11⅞ (22.5 x 30.1)
Estate seal embossed lower left in reverse

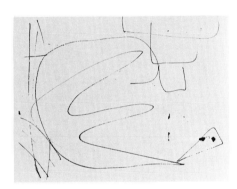

D456A. Pen and ink   [1950–53]
8⅞ x 11⅞ (22.5 x 30.1)
Estate seal embossed lower left in reverse

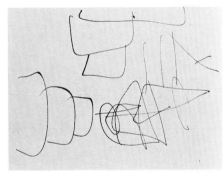

D457B. Pen and ink   [1950–53]
8⅞ x 11⅞ (22.5 x 30.1)
Estate seal embossed lower left in reverse

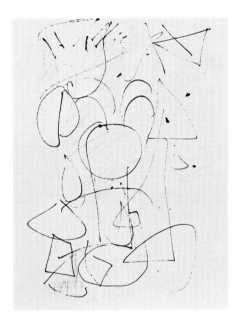

D459A. Pen and ink and colored
pencil   [1950–53]
11⅞ x 8⅞ (30.1 x 22.5)
Estate seal embossed lower left

D456B. Pen and ink   [1950–53]
8⅞ x 11⅞ (22.5 x 30.1)

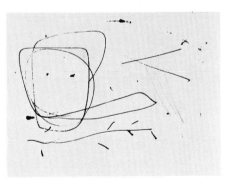

D458A. Pen and ink and colored
pencil   [1950–53]
8⅞ x 11⅞ (22.5 x 30.1)

D459B. Pen and ink   [1950–53]
8⅞ x 11⅞ (22.5 x 30.1)
Estate seal embossed lower left in reverse

D460A. Pen and ink and colored
pencil   [1950–53]
8⅞ x 11⅞ (22.5 x 30.1)

D460B. Pen and ink   [1950–53]
11⅞ x 8⅞ (30.1 x 22.5)
Estate seal embossed upper left in reverse

D462. Pencil   [1950–53]
10½ x 8¹⁄₁₆ (26.7 x 20.4)
Estate seal embossed lower left

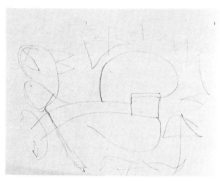

D463A. Pencil   [1950–53]
8¹⁄₁₆ x 10⁹⁄₁₆ (20.4 x 26.8)

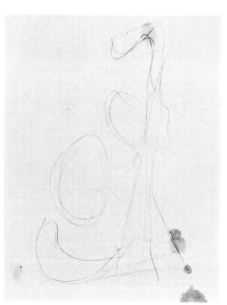

D461. Pencil   [1950–53]
10½ x 8¹⁄₁₆ (26.7 x 20.4)
Estate seal embossed lower left

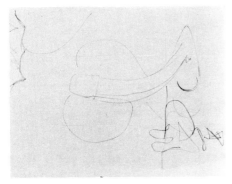

D463B. Pencil   [1950–53]
8¹/₁₆ x 10⁹/₁₆ (20.4 x 26.8)
Estate seal embossed lower left in reverse

D464A. Pencil   [1950–53]
8 x 10½ (20.4 x 26.7)

D464B. Pencil   [1950–53]
8 x 10½ (20.4 x 26.7)
Estate seal embossed lower left in reverse

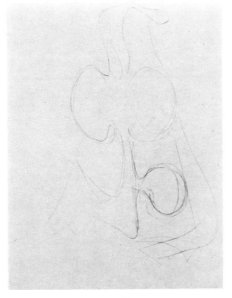

D465. Pencil   [1950–53]
10⁹/₁₆ x 8¹/₁₆ (26.7 x 20.4)
Estate seal embossed upper right

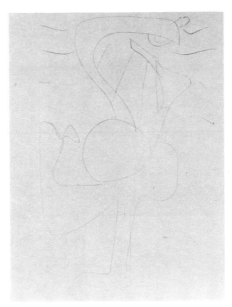

D466. Pencil   [1950–53]
10½ x 8¹/₁₆ (26.6 x 20.4)
Estate seal embossed lower left

D467. Pencil   [1950–53]
10⁹/₁₆ x 8¹/₁₆ (26.7 x 20.4)
Estate seal embossed lower left

D468. Pencil   [1950–53]
10½ x 8¹/₁₆ (26.6 x 20.4)
Estate seal embossed lower left

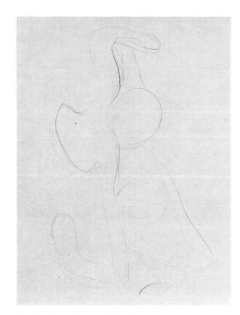

D469. Pencil   [1950–53]
10⁹/₁₆ x 8¹/₁₆ (26.7 x 20.4)
Estate seal embossed lower left

D470A. Ball-point pen and ink   [1950–53]
8³/₈ x 10¹⁵/₁₆ (21.2 x 27.7)

D470B. Ball-point pen and ink   [1950–53]
8³/₈ x 10¹⁵/₁₆ (21.2 x 27.7)
Estate seal embossed lower left in reverse

D471A. Ball-point pen and ink   [1950–53]
8³/₈ x 10¹⁵/₁₆ (21.2 x 27.7)

D471B. Ball-point pen and ink   [1950–53]
8³/₈ x 10¹⁵/₁₆ (21.2 x 27.7)
Estate seal embossed lower left in reverse

D472. Pencil   [1950–53]
8 x 5 (20.4 x 12.7)

D473. Pencil   [1950–53]
5 x 8 (12.7 x 20.3)

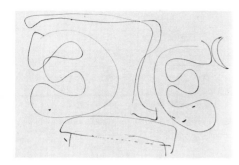

D474A. Pen and ink   [1950–53]
11¹⁵/₁₆ x 17¹³/₁₆ (30.2 x 45.2)

D474B. Pen and ink   [1950–53]
11¹⁵/₁₆ x 17¹³/₁₆ (30.2 x 45.2)
Estate seal embossed lower left in reverse

D475. Pen and ink and colored
pencil   [1950]
13⅞ x 11 (35.1 x 27.9)

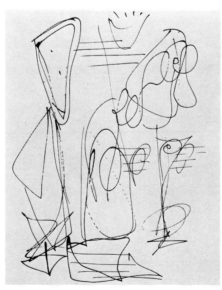

D476. Pen and ink   [1950]
13⅞ x 11 (35.1 x 27.9)

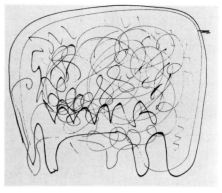

D477. Pen and ink   [1950]
11 x 13⅞ (27.9 x 35.1)

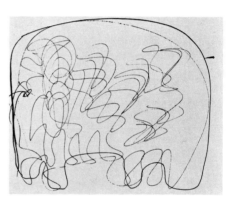

D478. Pen and ink   [1950]
11 x 13⅞ (27.9 x 35.1)

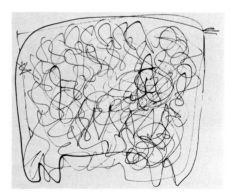

D479. Pen and ink   [1950]
11 x 13⅞ (27.9 x 35.1)

D480. Pen and ink   [1950]
11 x 13⅞ (27.9 x 35.1)

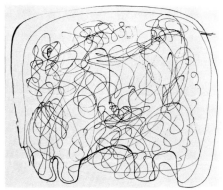

D483. Pen and ink   [1950]
11 x 13⅞ (27.9 x 35.1)

D486. Pen and ink   [1950]
13⅞ x 11 (35.1 x 27.9)
Estate seal embossed lower left

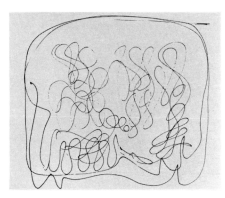

D481. Pen and ink   [1950]
11 x 13⅞ (27.9 x 35.1)

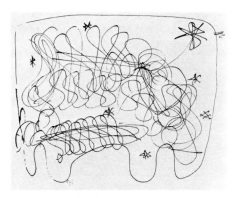

D484. Pen and ink   [1950]
11 x 13⅞ (27.9 x 35.1)

D487. Pen and ink   [1950]
13⅞ x 11 (35.1 x 27.9)
Estate seal embossed lower left

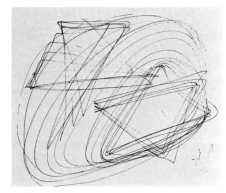

D482. Pen and ink   [1950]
11 x 13⅞ (27.9 x 35.1)

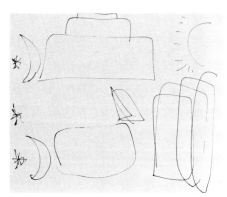

D485. Pen and ink   [1950]
11 x 13⅞ (27.9 x 35.1)

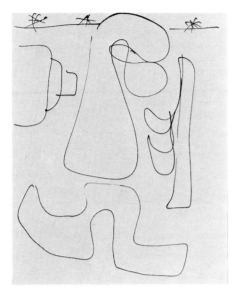

D488. Pen and ink   [1950]
13⅞ x 11 (35.1 x 27.9)
Estate seal embossed lower left

D490. Pen and ink   [1950]
13¹³/₁₆ x 11 (35.0 x 27.9)
Estate seal embossed lower left

D492. Pen and ink   [1948]
8⅝ x 11¾ (21.9 x 29.7)

D493. Pen and ink   [1948]
8⅝ x 11¾ (22.0 x 29.7)

D489. Pen and ink   [1950]
13⅞ x 11 (35.1 x 27.9)
Estate seal embossed lower left

D491. Pen and ink   [1950]
11 x 13⅞ (27.9 x 35.1)

D494. Pen and ink and gouache [1948–49]
Illustrated in color as frontispiece
23⁷/₈ x 18³/₄ (60.5 x 47.6)
Private collection

D497. Gouache [1938–40]
22⁷/₁₆ x 14¹³/₁₆ (56.9 x 37.6)

D498B. Chalk on paper 1939
26³/₁₆ x 17⁹/₁₆ (66.5 x 44.5)
Signed lower right in chalk: M. Louis 39
Estate seal embossed lower right in reverse

D495. Gouache [1940–45]
15³/₄ x 22¹³/₁₆ (39.9 x 57.9)

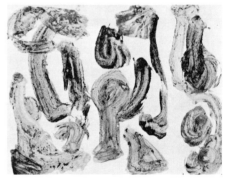

D498A. Gouache on paper 1940
17⁹/₁₆ x 26³/₁₆ (44.5 x 66.5)
Signed lower left in gouache: M Louis / -40-

D499. Gouache 1953
15⁵/₈ x 20³/₈ (39.7 x 51.7)
Signed lower center scratched: Louis 53

D496. Gouache [1940–45]
irregular: 19¹/₄ x 25¹/₄ (48.9 x 64.2)

D500. Gouache   1953
15⅝ x 20⅜ (39.7 x 51.7)
Signed lower right scratched: Louis 53

D501. Gouache   1941
17⅝ x 23¹⁵/₁₆ (44.8 x 60.8)
Signed lower right in gouache: ML 41

D502. Gouache   [1938–40]
15⅝ x 23¼ (39.7 x 59.0)

D503. Gouache   [1940–45]
16 x 22¾ (40.6 x 57.7)

#504. *Portrait of Stephens Berge*   circa 1930–34
pencil
Signed center right in pencil:
For Steve/Maurice
No estate seal
The Maryland Institute, College of Art,
Baltimore

#505. Pen and ink   1948
8¹¹/₁₆ x 11¾ (22.0 x 29.8)
Signed lower right in pencil: M Louis 48
No estate seal
Private collection

#506. Gouache   1948
15⅝ x 22¹¹/₁₆ (39.7 x 57.6)
Signed lower right in ink: M. Louis '48
No estate seal
Private collection

#507. Pen and ink   [1949]
dimensions not available
No estate seal
Andrew Bradford Smith, Chicago, Illinois

#508. Gouache   1953
26⅛ x 40 (66.3 x 101.6)
Signed lower left in pencil twice: Louis 53
No estate seal
William Spiegel, Baltimore, Maryland